STUDY GUIDE

Night

Elie Wiesel

WITH CONNECTIONS

HOLT, RINEHART AND WINSTON
Harcourt Brace & Company
Austin • New York • Orlando • Atlanta • San Francisco • Boston • Dallas • Toronto • London

Staff Credits

Director: Mescal Evler

Managing Editor: Bill Wahlgren

Executive Editor: Katie Vignery

Editors: M. Kathleen Judge, Boris Kolba

Editorial Staff: *Assistant Managing Editor,* Marie H. Price; *Copyediting Manager,* Michael Neibergall; *Senior Copyeditor,* Mary Malone; *Copyeditors,* Joel Bourgeois, Gabrielle Field, Suzi A. Hunn, Jane M. Kominek, Millicent Ondras, Theresa Reding, Désirée Reid, Kathleen Scheiner; *Editorial Operations Coordinator,* Lori De La Garza; *Editorial Coordinators,* Heather Cheyne, Mark Holland, Marcus Johnson, Jill O'Neal, Janet Riley; *Word Processors,* Ruth Hooker, Margaret Sanchez, Liz Dickson, Gail Coupland, Laura Kadjar

Permissions: Lee Noble, Catherine Paré

Design: Joe Melomo, *Design Director*

Prepress Production: Beth Prevelige, Simira Davis, Joan Lindsay

Manufacturing Coordinator: Michael Roche

Cover Illustration: Joe Melomo

For permission to reprint copyrighted material, grateful acknowledgment is made to the following source:

Hill and Wang, a division of Farrar, Straus & Giroux, Inc.: From *Night* by Elie Wiesel, translated by Stella Rodway. Translation copyright © 1960 by MacGibbon and Kee; copyright renewed © 1988 by The Collins Publishing Group. All rights reserved.

Printed in the United States of America

ISBN 0-03-055432-2

456 085 03 02

TABLE *of* CONTENTS

Using This Study Guide

Approaching the Book

The successful study of a book often depends on students' enthusiasm, curiosity, and openness. The ideas in **Introducing the Book** will help you create such a climate for your class. Background information in **About the Writer** and **About the Book** can also be used to pique students' interest.

Reading and Responding to the Book

Making Meanings questions are designed for both individual response and group or class discussion. They range from personal response to high-level critical thinking.

Reading Strategies worksheets contain graphic organizers. They help students explore techniques that enhance both comprehension and literary analysis. Many worksheets are appropriate for more than one set of chapters.

Book Notes provide high-interest information relating to historical, cultural, literary, and other elements of the book. The **Investigate** questions and **Reader's Log** ideas guide students to further research and consideration.

Choices suggest a wide variety of activities for exploring different aspects of the book, either individually or collaboratively. The results may be included in a portfolio or used as springboards for larger projects.

Glossary and Vocabulary (1) clarifies allusions and other references and (2) provides definitions students may refer to as they read. The **Vocabulary Worksheets** activities are based on the Vocabulary Words.

Reader's Log, Double-Entry Journal, and **Group Discussion Log** model formats and spark ideas for responding to the book. These pages are designed to be a resource for independent reading as well.

Responding to the Book as a Whole

The following features provide options for culminating activities that can be used in whole-class, small-group, or independent-study situations.

Book Review provides a format for summarizing and integrating the major literary elements.

Book Projects suggest multiple options for culminating activities. **Writing About the Book, Cross-Curricular Connections,** and **Multimedia and Internet Connections** propose project options that extend the text into other genres, content areas, and environments.

Responding to the Connections

Making Meanings questions in **Exploring the Connections** facilitate discussion of the additional readings in the HRW LIBRARY edition of this book.

This Study Guide is intended to

- *provide maximum versatility and flexibility*
- *serve as a ready resource for background information on both the author and the book*
- *act as a catalyst for discussion, analysis, interpretation, activities, and further research*
- *provide reproducible masters that can be used for either individual or collaborative work, including discussions and projects*
- *provide multiple options for evaluating students' progress through the novel and the Connections*

Literary Elements

- plot structure
- major themes
- characterization
- setting
- point of view
- symbolism, irony, and other elements appropriate to the title

Making Meanings Reproducible Masters

- First Thoughts
- Shaping Interpretations
- Connecting with the Text
- Extending the Text
- Challenging the Text

A **Reading Check** focuses on review and comprehension.

The Worksheets Reproducible Masters

- Reading Strategies Worksheets
- Literary Elements Worksheets
- Vocabulary Worksheets

Reaching All Students

Most classrooms include students from a variety of backgrounds and with a range of learning styles. The questions and activities in this Study Guide have been developed to meet diverse student interests, abilities, and learning styles. Of course, students are full of surprises, and a question or activity that is challenging to an advanced student can also be handled successfully by students who are less proficient readers. The interest level, flexibility, and variety of these questions and activities make them appropriate for a range of students.

Struggling Readers and Students with Limited English Proficiency: The **Making Meanings** questions, the **Choices** activities, and the **Reading Strategies** worksheets all provide opportunities for students to check their understanding of the text and to review their reading. The **Book Projects** ideas are designed for a range of student abilities and learning styles. Both questions and activities motivate and encourage students to make connections to their own interests and experiences. The **Vocabulary Worksheets** can be used to facilitate language acquisition. **Dialogue Journals,** with you the teacher or with more advanced students as respondents, can be especially helpful to these students.

Advanced Students: The writing opportunity suggested with the **Making Meanings** questions and the additional research suggestions in **Book Notes** should offer a challenge to these students. The **Choices** and **Book Projects** activities can be taken to advanced levels. **Dialogue Journals** allow advanced students to act as mentors or to engage each other intellectually.

Auditory Learners: A range of suggestions in this Study Guide targets students who respond particularly well to auditory stimuli: making and listening to audiotapes and engaging in class discussion, role-playing, debate, oral reading, and oral presentation. See **Making Meanings** questions, **Choices,** and **Book Projects** options (especially **Cross-Curricular Connections** and **Multimedia and Internet Connections**).

Visual/Spatial Learners: Students are guided to create visual representations of text scenes and concepts and to analyze films or videos in **Choices** and in **Book Projects.** The **Reading Strategies** and **Literary Elements Worksheets** utilize graphic organizers as a way to both assimilate and express information.

Tactile/Kinesthetic Learners: The numerous interactive, hands-on, and problem-solving projects are designed to encourage the involvement of students motivated by action and movement. The projects also provide an opportunity for **interpersonal learners** to connect with others through book-related tasks. The **Group Discussion Log** will help students track the significant points of their interactions.

Verbal Learners: For students who naturally connect to the written and spoken word, the **Reader's Logs** and **Dialogue Journals** will have particular appeal. This Study Guide offers numerous writing opportunities: See **Making Meanings, Choices, Book Notes,** and **Writing About the Book** in **Book Projects.** These options should also be attractive to **intrapersonal learners.**

Assessment Options

Perhaps the most important goal of assessment is to provide feedback on the effectiveness of instructional strategies. As you monitor the degree to which your students understand and engage with the book, you will naturally adjust the frequency and ratio of class to small-group and verbal to nonverbal activities, as well as the extent to which direct teaching of reading strategies, literary elements, or vocabulary is appropriate to your students' needs.

If you are in an environment where **portfolios** contain only carefully chosen samples of students' writing, you may want to introduce a second, "working," portfolio and negotiate grades with students after examining all or selected items from this portfolio.

The features in this Study Guide are designed to facilitate a variety of assessment techniques.

Reader's Logs and Double-Entry Journals can be briefly reviewed and responded to (students may wish to indicate entries they would prefer to keep private). The logs and journals are an excellent measure of students' engagement with and understanding of the book.

Group Discussion Log entries provide students with an opportunity for self-evaluation of their participation in both book discussions and project planning.

Making Meanings questions allow you to observe and evaluate a range of student responses. Those who have difficulty with literal and interpretive questions may respond more completely to **Connecting** and **Extending**. The **Writing Opportunity** provides you with the option of ongoing assessment: You can provide feedback to students' brief written responses to these prompts as they progress through the book.

Reading Strategies Worksheets, Book Review, and Literary Elements Worksheets lend themselves well to both quick assessment and students' self-evaluation. They can be completed collaboratively and the results shared with the class, or students can compare their individual responses in a small-group environment.

Choices activities and writing prompts offer all students the chance to successfully complete an activity, either individually or collaboratively, and share the results with the class. These items are ideal for peer evaluation and can help prepare students for presenting and evaluating larger projects at the completion of the book unit.

Vocabulary Worksheets can be used as diagnostic tools or as part of a concluding test.

Book Projects evaluations might be based on the degree of understanding of the book demonstrated by the project. Students' presentations of their projects should be taken into account, and both self-evaluation and peer evaluation can enter into the overall assessment.

The **Test** is a traditional assessment tool in three parts: objective items, short-answer questions, and essay questions.

Questions for Self-evaluation and Goal Setting

- What are the three most important things I learned in my work with this book?
- How will I follow up so that I remember them?
- What was the most difficult part of working with this book?
- How did I deal with the difficulty, and what would I do differently?
- What two goals will I work toward in my reading, writing, group, and other work?
- What steps will I take to achieve those goals?

Items for a "Working" Portfolio

- reading records
- drafts of written work and project plans
- audio- and videotapes of presentations
- notes on discussions
- reminders of cooperative projects, such as planning and discussion notes
- artwork
- objects and mementos connected with themes and topics in the book
- other evidence of engagement with the book

For help with establishing and maintaining portfolio assessment, examine the **Portfolio Management System** in ELEMENTS OF LITERATURE.

Answer Key

The Answer Key at the back of this guide is not intended to be definitive or to set up a right-wrong dichotomy. In questions that involve interpretation, however, students' responses should be defended by citations from the text.

Guidelines for Teaching About the Holocaust: Summary

The following is a summary from Guidelines for Teaching About the Holocaust, *a document produced by the United States Holocaust Memorial Museum. The Museum's primary mission is to promote education about the history of the Holocaust and to foster an understanding of the implications of this event for today. A study of the history of the Holocaust can be a unit of study in itself, or it can be incorporated into existing courses in the school's curriculum, such as United States History, World History, World Cultures, Government, Art and Art History, and Contemporary World Problems. Sample curricula and lesson plans have been collected by the Museum.*

The complete Guidelines *appear on p. 83 of this Study Guide. For information from the Museum, please contact:*

Education Department
United States Holocaust Memorial Museum
100 Raoul Wallenberg Place, SW
Washington, DC 20024
Telephone: (202) 488-0400

Teaching About the Holocaust Through Literature*

The following is a brief outline of the major points which should be considered when teaching about the Holocaust.

1. The Holocaust was a crucial event in the history of humanity. A study of its literature can lead students to examine basic moral issues, patterns of human behavior, and the human capacity for evil. Students can come to realize:

- the importance of democratic institutions
- the need to respect the rights of others
- the value of a pluralistic society
- the ramifications of prejudice, racism, and stereotyping
- the need for individual responsibility and action in the face of oppression, abuse of power, violation of civil rights, and destructive uses of technology

- the historical, social, religious, political, and economic factors which can contribute to the destruction of civilized values

2. The following are to be considered when creating the lessons for a study of the Holocaust.

- Define the Holocaust as a specific event in twentieth-century history. Place the events and people of the Holocaust within their proper historical context. Emphasize the importance of decisions made by individuals, groups, and nations that led to the Holocaust. Such an event is not inevitable—its history can be traced and responsibility for actions and events assigned.

- Use a broad range of literary genres: novels, short stories, drama, poetry, diaries, and memoirs.

- Highlight different policies carried out by Nazis towards various groups of people; avoid, however, using the information as a basis for a comparison of suffering between groups.

- Do not oversimplify the difficult questions and complicated answers that are raised in a study of the Holocaust.

- Learning activities must engage the interest of the students, foster critical analysis, and provoke thought. Simulation exercises are to be avoided as they trivialize the experience and fail to keep students focused on the central issues.

- Use precise language to clarify terms and avoid distortion of fact. Teach students to recognize strategies that corrupt language and bend it to particular agendas.

- Instruct and give your students practice in analyzing and interpreting sources of information. Teach them to distinguish between fact, opinion, and fiction; primary and secondary sources; and types of evidence such as court testimonies, oral histories, and autobiographical testimonies.

*Adaptation of "Guidelines for Teaching About the Holocaust" (retitled "Teaching About the Holocaust Through Literature") by William S. Parsons and Samuel Totten. Reprinted by permission of **United States Holocaust Memorial Museum.***

- Teach students to recognize and avoid stereotypical descriptions, to avoid romanticizing events and people, and to strive for a balance in perspective.
- Personalize the statistics of the Holocaust.
- Use appropriate written and audiovisual content.

Adapted from **Guidelines for Teaching About the Holocaust,** *by the United States Holocaust Memorial Museum.*

About the Writer

More on Wiesel

Abrahamson, Irving, ed. **Against Silence: The Voice and Vision of Elie Wiesel.** New York: Holocaust Library, 1985.

Cargas, Harry James. **Telling the Tale: A Tribute to Elie Wiesel on the Occasion of His 65th Birthday: Essays, Reflections, and Poems.** St. Louis: Time Being Books, 1993.

Fine, Ellen S. **Legacy of Night: The Literary Universe of Elie Wiesel.** Albany: State University of New York Press, 1982.

Pariser, Michael. **Elie Wiesel: Bearing Witness.** Brookfield, CT: Millbrook Press, 1994.

Rittner, Carol, ed. **Elie Wiesel: Between Memory and Hope.** New York: NYU Press, 1992.

Stern, Ellen N. **Elie Wiesel: A Voice for Humanity.** Philadelphia: Jewish Publication Society, 1996.

Wiesel, Elie, and Alan C. Rosen, eds. **Celebrating Elie Wiesel: Stories, Essays, Reflections.** Notre Dame, IN: University of Notre Dame Press, 1998.

Also by Wiesel

Dawn (1961)

A Beggar in Jerusalem (1970)

A Jew Today (1978)

The Testament (1981)

The Fifth Son (1985)

Night/Dawn/Day (1985)

The Forgotten (1992)

From the Kingdom of Memory: Reminiscences (1990)

All Rivers Run to the Sea: Memoirs (1995)

Children of Job: American Second-Generation Witnesses to the Holocaust (1997), with Alan Berger

A biography of Wiesel appears in **Night**, *HRW LIBRARY edition. You may wish to share this additional biographical information with your students.*

On April 11, 1945, American soldiers entered the Buchenwald concentration camp, and the horrible suffering they found there made them weep. Among the prisoners still alive at the camp was a sixteen-year-old Jewish boy from a small village in Hungary. Escorted by his American liberators, the boy walked out of Buchenwald. The young boy grew up to be one of the world's most respected authors, lecturers, teachers, and activists for peace. The boy was Elie Wiesel.

Eliezer Wiesel was born September 30, 1928, into the close-knit Jewish family of his mother Sarah, his father Shlomo, and his three sisters. As a very young child, Wiesel was interested in becoming a rabbi. He was fascinated by sacred Jewish texts and participated in long discussions with elders about God. He was disillusioned while still a child. Less than a year after German soldiers occupied Sighet, the village where he lived, Wiesel was plunged into one of the longest nights of the twentieth century. Ultimately his mother and youngest sister perished, along with thousands of others in the Auschwitz camp, and his father died of beatings, starvation, and dysentery in Buchenwald only months before the American soldiers arrived.

After liberation, Elie Wiesel lived in a French orphanage for several years. In Paris, one of his sisters recognized his photo in a newspaper story about the orphanage. Two of Wiesel's sisters had survived, and the three were reunited. Wiesel entered the Sorbonne in 1948 and then worked as a journalist for newspapers in France and for the Israeli daily *Yediot Achronot*. For ten years after his liberation from Buchenwald, Wiesel maintained a personal vow of silence regarding his Holocaust experience. Then, in 1954, Wiesel interviewed the Nobel laureate writer François Mauriac. When Mauriac told Wiesel that he could never forget the description of Jewish children torn from their mothers and deported to unimaginable horror, Wiesel told Mauriac, "I was one of them." The older man encouraged Wiesel to break his vow of silence—to write about his Holocaust experience. The first version of *Night* appeared in 1956 as an eight-hundred-page memoir, written in Yiddish, published in Argentina, and titled *Un di Welt Hot Geshvign (And the World Kept Silent)*. Wiesel then compressed his memoir into an autobiographical novel in French, *La Nuit (Night)*, of just over one hundred pages. After drastic rewrites and difficulties finding a publisher who would work with his text—often considered too depressing or too harrowing—*La Nuit* finally appeared in 1958. American publisher Hill & Wang, which bought Wiesel's manuscript for one hundred dollars, published the English-language version two years later. *Night* sold only a few thousand copies in its first years in print. Its sales now have exceeded one million copies.

Elie Wiesel has written more than thirty-five books since *Night.* He writes his books first in French, and his wife translates them into English. Often writing about victims of oppression, Wiesel is determined to give meaning to the absurdities of the past: "[I have a] conviction that man must impose a meaning upon events that perhaps have none. . . . I am absolutely convinced that even when faith is impossible you must make it possible." Elie Wiesel, now an American citizen and professor at Boston University, is one of the most significant writers addressing the Holocaust. He is considered by many to be the most eloquent witness to World War II.

Special Considerations

Possible sensitive issues in this book include graphic descriptions of murder and abuse of corpses, including those of children, and incidents of extreme brutality, temporary insanity, and emotional unbalance.

NOTE: *Many film, video, and internet resources include graphic images of Nazi atrocities. Review all films and videos before showing them to students, and provide students with as much guidance as possible when using the Internet.*

For Viewing

The Holocaust: In Memory of Millions. Bethesda, MD: Discovery Communications, 1993. Walter Cronkite narrates and hosts this interview with Elie Wiesel.

A Portrait of Elie Wiesel: In the Shadow of Flames. Alexandria, VA: PBS Video, 1989. An interview with the author accompanied by artwork and photographs that illustrate his memories of childhood and complement his comments on his writing and philosophy.

For Listening

All Rivers Run to the Sea. New York: Random House Audio, 1995. Elie Wiesel reads from his memoir.

Elie Wiesel at the National Press Club. Washington, DC: National Public Radio, 1983. A recording of Wiesel's discussion of the role of journalism during World War II and his own mission as a writer.

Historical Context

After World War I, conditions in Germany were chaotic, making the country susceptible to Adolf Hitler and the goals of his Nazi party. The German mark was almost worthless after massive reparations payments weakened the economy and an industrial strike caused an economic crisis. Germans resented bitterly the humiliating terms of the Treaty of Versailles, which had ended the first World War. The German government was one of the most liberal in the world, but the Germans had little experience with democracy, and many middle- and upper-class citizens who had lived comfortably under the old monarchy feared the newly formed government. For these reasons, the country remained in nearly constant turmoil. Many Germans blamed Jews, Marxists, and the "November Criminals" who signed the treaty.

This unstable political and economic situation made it easier for extremist political groups to rise to power. One of these was the German Workers' Party, a small discussion group in Munich. The German army hired a World War I veteran named Adolf Hitler to investigate this small political organization. While infiltrating the group, Hitler became interested in expressing his own political views and joined the party. Hitler's aims were mainly focused on Germany's national interests, but he also promised the German people military conquest and social revolution. The wealthy were attracted by his opposition to communism, and the powerless responded to his ideas of racial superiority.

Renamed the National Socialist German Workers Party (in German, *Nationalsozialistische Deutsche Arbeiterpartei*), the Nazis made Hitler their leader. Hitler discovered his talent for oratory and, in 1923, he planned an attempt (which was later aborted) to take over the Bavarian government. During his resulting nine-month imprisonment for treason, Hitler dictated the text of *Mein Kampf (My Struggle)* to his aide Rudolf Hess. *Mein Kampf* set forth his plan to conquer much of Europe and spelled out his philosophy of racial superiority. Hitler blamed the Jews for all world evils: "By defending myself against the Jews, I am doing the Lord's work." He also attacked democracy, stating that it would inevitably lead to communism.

With Hitler as their spokesperson, the Nazis continued to gain support from the German population. In 1930, Hitler campaigned extensively throughout the country and toned down his antisemitic speeches (which had failed to attract votes). In 1932, the Nazis became the dominant party in parliament. Through a series of political deals, Hitler forced the eighty-five-year-old president, Paul von Hindenburg, to name him chancellor in January 1933. By March of that year, Hitler had made himself dictator. Hitler seized control over the entire country and began his program of nationalism, racism, and aggression; in the first year, he opened Dachau, established the Gestapo (the secret police), and outlawed all press and all political parties.

Immediately, the Nazis began to revoke Jewish citizenship rights. The notorious 1935 Nuremberg Race Laws stripped German Jews of their citizenship, making them subjects of the Reich. Jews were forbidden to marry "Aryans" (blond-haired, blue-eyed, and of Germanic heritage). Later they were ordered to wear the yellow star of David on their clothing as identification. In 1938, the Nazis carried out the *Kristallnacht,* a coordinated mass rampage against Jewish people, homes, and synagogues in Germany and Austria.

Adolf Eichmann and Heydrich Reinhard were placed in charge of planning and conducting the *Endlösung* (Final Solution), or systematic elimination of Jews throughout Europe. The *Einsatzgruppen,* Nazi killing squads, rounded up thousands of Jews, forced them to dig mass graves, and then shot them. The Nazis began to assemble Jewish people in Germany and in the occupied countries into ghettos near railway stations—where they could be efficiently deported to camps. They were sent either to concentration camps where they worked as slave laborers, or to extermination camps where they were killed. Germany's 1939 invasion of Poland was the act of aggression that provoked England and France to declare a war that would eventually liberate the persecuted Jews. However, by the middle of 1940, the German army had conquered Denmark, Norway, Belgium, the Netherlands, Luxembourg, and France. The next year, Germany attacked Yugoslavia, Greece,

and the Soviet Union and in 1944, Hungary. The United States entered the war on December 8, 1941.

By 1944, the German army's situation had deteriorated. As the Russians pushed westward toward Germany, the Nazis began abandoning the camps along the eastern front, sometimes forcing concentration camp prisoners to march hundreds of miles in bitter winter weather. In April 1945, American soldiers entered Buchenwald; that same month, Adolf Hitler committed suicide inside his Berlin bunker.

When the war was finally over, the Nuremberg Trials of Nazi war criminals began. The International Military Tribunal conducted the first trial from November 1945 to October 1946. Twenty-two people, including chief Nazi advisors, diplomats, and military leaders, were tried for crimes against peace and humanity and for the murder of over six million Jews and five million other Europeans. Twelve more trials took place at Nuremberg from 1946 to 1949, involving more than 185 defendants. The trials have been criticized by some people for being too harsh or too vengeful. On the other hand, they were successful in establishing two things: They documented the crimes which occurred during the Holocaust, and set a new moral standard for soldiers and citizens by stating that people have a duty to refuse to carry out inhumane orders.

Israeli agents who specialized in bringing former Nazis to justice captured one of the primary architects of the Holocaust, Adolf Eichmann, in Argentina in 1960. After Eichmann's trial, the Israeli government sentenced him to death, executing him in 1962. Another Nazi fugitive was Josef Mengele, the "Angel of Death" of Auschwitz. This German doctor, who conducted horrible experiments on inmates, escaped to South America. He evaded the German warrant for his arrest until he died in 1979; his remains were buried under a false name, but DNA testing in the 1980s proved that the remains were those of Mengele.

Literary Context

Elie Wiesel's Nobel Prize acceptance speech reminds us that the literature of the Holocaust began even while the Holocaust was at its height, in the testimonial writings of concentration camp inmates and other targets of Nazi aggression. One of the most significant events of this century, the Holocaust has generated a massive creative response in the visual arts, music, theater, and literature. The tens of thousands of survivor testimonies lie at the core of Holocaust literature. Many were personal thoughts written for private reading by family members; others (like *Night*) were testimonies intended for a wider public. Although many of these testimonies have been lost or forgotten, the extant records of witnesses constitute an array of literature which can be placed under the label of "Holocaust writings."

Some Holocaust writers have a prominent role in the literary world. These first-generation writers include important artists and intellectuals such as Primo Levi, Viktor Frankl, philosopher Hannah Arendt, and novelist Jerzy Kosinski. It is not surprising that comparisons have been made between *Night* and Anne Frank's *Diary of a Young Girl*. Though both are accounts of the Holocaust as experienced by youths, the events described by the authors are fundamentally different. Frank relates efforts to avoid capture; Weisel relates efforts to survive after capture.

The children of Holocaust survivors, the "second generation," have also begun to sort through their own experiences. Unable to recall the Holocaust directly, they have grown up in families with histories so horrible that the older generations often remain silent. Years later, the Holocaust continues to have profound effects on the personal and cultural identity of these writers.

Wiesel, after living and studying in France, was greatly influenced by the French existential writers and philosophers. He developed a writing style that is stark and direct. As do the philosophical fictions of Albert Camus, Jean-Paul Sartre, and André Malraux, Wiesel's experimental narratives often evade the linear chronology of a typical novel, and his works do not rely on detailed visual imagery. A minimalist, Wiesel attempts to express himself succinctly: "Writing is more like sculpture where you remove, you eliminate in order to make the work visible. Even those pages you remove somehow remain."

Wiesel, in keeping with the existentialists, addresses moral issues; he explores the meaning of life in a society without God, and he tries to reconstruct a hope in humanity. This surfaces in his themes of guilt, hypocrisy, silence, and, most importantly, apathy. For Wiesel, apathy is the greatest crime of all—his life motto is, "Indifference to evil is evil." Although humans are trapped in an absurd world, Wiesel asserts that people are responsible for the moral choices they make. As does Camus, he considers the most offensive person to be the one who sits on the fence.

The unique horror of the Holocaust makes it difficult to assess the literary merit of World War II literature by conventional aesthetic standards. Before the Holocaust, writers used their art to explore human meaning and purpose, but the reality of the Holocaust, and the magnitude of its crimes against humanity, challenged the whole tradition of Western thought and art. According to critic Irving Howe:

> The Italian-Jewish writer Primo Levi, soon after arriving at Auschwitz, was told by a Nazi guard: "Hier ist kein warum" ("Here there is no why, here nothing need be explained"). This passing observation by a shrewd thug provides as good an insight into the world of the camps as anything found in the entire scholarly literature.

Problematic though it may be to use the intellectual and aesthetic resources of Western civilization to make sense of experiences that defy logic or morality, writers addressing the Holocaust still try. Many look back and attempt to find a purpose in it, often providing theories on how such horror might give birth to something good.

If the usual standards of literary criticism fail to apply to these stories, how do we decide their merit from a literary standpoint? A literary experience usually gives aesthetic satisfaction but, according to scholar Theodor Adorno, this type of satisfaction would blaspheme the testimonies. The effort to understand the literary significance of the Holocaust testimonies raises other questions. Who has the right to judge the stories of people who have endured such harrowing experiences? Can anyone but those who were there write legitimately about the Holocaust?

Critical Responses

"Wiesel is by far the most significant writer to have made the Holocaust the major theme of his work, even as it has been of central importance to his life. Thus, no historian, philosopher, theologian, or literary critic making any attempt at all to comprehend our time, our past, or our future can afford to ignore either the man or his work,"* wrote Irving Abrahamson in his edited collection *Against Silence: The Voice and Vision of Elie Wiesel.*

Wiesel's literary corpus is vast, encompassing memoirs, novels, short stories, essays, and poetry. With the exception of *Night,* Wiesel has produced very few directly autobiographical works. His Holocaust experience informs everything he writes, however, as do his Jewish heritage and identity. In this way, one can consider all of his works to be, in a certain sense, autobiographical. Yet, Daniel Stern commented, "Not since Albert Camus has there been such an eloquent spokesman for man."

Of *Night,* Lawrence L. Langer wrote:

> [A]t its heart lies the profoundest symbolic confrontation of our century, the meeting of man and Auschwitz—and this confrontation in turn confirms the defeat of man's tragic potentiality in our time, and the triumph of death in its most nihilistic guise. . . .
>
> "The Dominion of Death," in *Responses to Elie Wiesel*

Finally, perhaps ultimately, Wiesel is preoccupied with issues of theology, the relationship between people and God. "Of course, I go on quarreling with God. If I were to tell you that I believe in God the way I believed when I was a child, I would lie to you. If I would tell you I do not believe at all, I would lie, too. I am still searching for a possibility, for an answer." While readers can appreciate Wiesel's writing specifically as literature, the scope of his work also requires them to cross intellectual boundaries into the other disciplines of history, philosophy, and theology. Abrahamson wrote, "Wiesel's complete honesty, his truth, the profundity of his themes, and the skill with which he treats them—all combine magically to create what is for many a matchless experience. Wiesel has the capacity of fusing history and philosophy, art and morality, into masterworks that reach unfailingly into the very center of one's being." *

*From Preface and "quote dated December 31, 1978" from *Against Silence: The Voice and Vision of Elie Wiesel,* edited by Irving Abrahamson. Copyright © 1985 by Irving Abrahamson. Reprinted by permission of **United States Holocaust Memorial Museum.**

Plot and Setting

Elie Wiesel's *Night* is a personal account of the Holocaust. The memoir begins in 1941 in the Hungarian town of Sighet, where the young Wiesel lives with his family. The arrival of German soldiers in 1944 brings the Jewish residents of Sighet face to face with the war. First they are transferred to ghettos in Sighet, and then they are taken by train to the concentration camps. Events in Wiesel's book cover his experiences in Birkenau-Auschwitz, Buna, and Buchenwald.

Structure and Point of View

Night is a memoir told chronologically. Wiesel relates his concentration camp experiences in the first-person point of view. The reader can easily forget that this is the story of a teenager because of Eliezer's loss of innocence and faith in the face of evil. The narrator struggles like an adult to save his father's life, as well as his own. The book was written ten years after the events described and includes brief commentary by the author on events that occurred after his release.

Characters

Eliezer begins the book as a devout Jewish boy, the only son in a well-respected family. His experiences in the ghettos and in the camps transform him into a faithless survivor, an orphan, physically alive but emotionally dead.

Chlomo Wiesel, Eliezer's father, is a man of good standing in the Sighet Jewish community. Eliezer describes him as emotionally distant from his family and faith.

Moché the Beadle is a wise but poor man whom young Eliezer chooses as his instructor in the mystical tradition of their faith. Moché survives a Nazi massacre in 1942 and returns to warn the Jews of Sighet, but they will not believe his story.

Fellow prisoners in the camps reflect the complexity of human response to the duress of the concentration camp experience. These people include **Madame Schächter,** who loses her mind during the train transport and screams out her hysterical visions of fire; **Akibe Drumer,** who encourages others by singing Hasidic melodies but eventually loses his faith in the face of his selection for imminent death; **Rabbi Eliahou,** a good man who searches in vain for his beloved son; and **Juliek,** a Polish boy whose violin playing gives a few moments of solace to the suffering.

Themes

Self-preservation versus family commitment: The responsibility to one's self is instinctual and can conflict with one's responsibility to others, even family members. The narrator illustrates this through the presentation of the changing relationships between sons and fathers, describing how fathers and sons struggle to maintain their relationships.

Dignity in the face of inhuman cruelty: The moments of compassion, continued observances of religious obligations, and other acts of humanity may seem insignificant compared to the acts of indignity heaped upon the prisoners in the camp (by the Nazis and by one another), yet these expressions of goodness enabled prisoners to sustain a sense of human dignity.

Struggle to maintain faith: The daily presence of death and the terror of "selection" force the issue of faith on once-devout Eliezer and on all of the prisoners victimized because they are Jews.

Emotional death: "From the depths of the mirror, a corpse gazed back at me." Physical survival in *Night* does not indicate that one has avoided death, as Moché the Beadle's return to Sighet and the last lines of the memoir illustrate.

A **Literary Elements Worksheet** focusing on **theme** appears on page 45 of this Study Guide.

Motifs

Two visual motifs dominate the memoir. **Night** and imagery associated with nighttime recur throughout this story, which is one of "the long dark night of the soul" for Elie Wiesel and the twentieth century. **Eyes,** often considered the windows of the soul, are Wiesel's device for characterizing the personality or emotional health of those he encounters.

A **Literary Elements Worksheet** focusing on **motif** appears on page 44 of this Study Guide.

Tone

Tone is the attitude of the writer toward the subject matter. For Wiesel, tone may have presented a difficult struggle. It took him many years to gain enough distance from his subject matter to be able to write about it at all. The tone he achieves in *Night* might be described in one or more of the following ways: personal yet objective, restrained, unadorned, documentary-like, quietly dignified, helpless, mournful, profoundly sad.

A **Literary Elements Worksheet** focusing on **tone** appears on page 46 of this Study Guide.

Options

Engaging Issues

While the realities of the Holocaust cannot be compared to everyday experiences of pain, camaraderie, suffering, or even death, a study of the Holocaust can raise issues of individual choices and responsible citizenship. The following exercise was created as part of the educational program at Holocaust Museum Houston.

THE TRIANGLE*

Which Role Would You Choose?

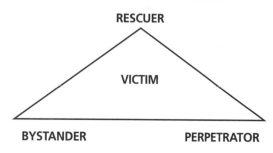

Objective: Students will learn the varying roles of individuals in the Holocaust to better understand their behavior in their everyday lives.

European Jews, along with other people who were considered "not good enough to live among Hitler's Aryan people," were targeted with death during the Holocaust. These people were *victims* and although innocent, they had no choice regarding their selection to be persecuted. It is important to understand that all the other individuals were in a position to choose the role they wished to follow in the Holocaust. People chose to be either *perpetrators, rescuers,* or *bystanders.* About ten percent of the population chose to be *perpetrators.* Less than five percent chose to be *rescuers.* Most people chose the role of *bystanders.*

Questions

- What occurrences during this time period influenced individual decisions as to the roles they selected?
- Why do you believe so few decided to be *Rescuers?*

- What qualities do you believe the *Rescuers* had?
- What qualities do you believe the *Perpetrators* possessed?
- What changes do you think would have occurred during this time period if the *Bystanders* had helped the *Rescuers* in the war against the *Perpetrators?*
- What percentage of people today play the role of the *Bystander* when a decision has to be made?
- Which role do you choose today in a conflict situation? Why?

Students should answer these questions individually, then discuss them in the context of this quotation:

"The World is too dangerous to live in—not because of the people who do evil, but because of the people who sit and let it happen."†—Albert Einstein

DRAMATIC READING

Holocaust Memoirs

Thousands of people who survived the Holocaust have written memoirs about their experiences. You can find many of these in any library. Split the class into groups of four to six students each. Each student in the group should choose a memoir of a Holocaust survivor and select several passages that are most meaningful. The passages should be shared with the class.

*"The Triangle." Copyright © by **The Holocaust Museum Houston.** Reprinted by permission of the publisher.

†Quote by Albert Einstein. Copyright © by the **Philosophical Library.** Reprinted by permission of the publisher.

Holocaust Museums

Many cities and states have established museums to commemorate the people who suffered and died in the Holocaust. The federal government has created the United States Holocaust Memorial Museum in Washington, D.C. In Europe, memorials exist at several of the concentration camp sites. Ask students to use the Internet to make a directory of six to eight of the Holocaust museums or memorials. Have them begin with the United States Holocaust Memorial Museum, the Simon Wiesenthal Center's Museum of Tolerance, and the Holocaust Museum Houston. Students should give the location and contact information for each one. They may be able to take a virtual tour of the museum or simply glean information from the site and share it with the class.

Graphic photographs depicting Nazi atrocities can be found on the Internet. Provide students with as much guidance as possible.

Video Feed

Introduce students to the circumstances leading up to the Holocaust or to the experiences of concentration camp survivors.

- *The Rise and Fall of Adolf Hitler,* a set of six videotapes produced by ZDF and A&E (1995), is a psychological biography of Adolf Hitler.
- *Survivors of the Holocaust,* a Steven Spielberg production (1995), is a brief collection of some of the many video-taped memoirs recorded through the Survivors of the Shoah Foundation. These memories are intercut with archival footage.

Face to Face

For some classroom audiences, it may be appropriate to introduce Jewish culture along with an introduction to World War II and the Holocaust. Contact a local temple or synagogue to inquire about a guest lecturer qualified to speak about the Jewish faith, the Hasidic tradition, the cabbala, and the Holocaust. If possible, arrange a trip to the synagogue or temple for this lesson.

Plot Synopsis and Literary Elements

Part I: Sighet to Birkenau

Plot Synopsis

Twelve-year-old Eliezer lives with his father, mother, and three sisters in the Hungarian village of Sighet. It is 1941. Devout in his Jewish faith, Eliezer dreams of becoming a rabbi. For hours he talks about the mysteries of God with Moché the Beadle, a *shammas*, or man with minor official duties at the synagogue, whom Eliezer chooses to be his instructor in the cabalistic books.

One day the non-Hungarian Jews of Sighet are deported. Moché is one of them. Later he returns to the village and tells the villagers how the Gestapo forced the prisoners to dig huge graves in the forest, then began killing them all. Wounded and taken for dead, Moché escaped back to Sighet. He tells the Jews of Sighet what happened, but no one believes him. They think the German army will be defeated soon.

The Germans, however, come to Sighet, and on the seventh day of Passover, they arrest the leaders of the Jewish community. The soldiers force the Jews into two small ghettos: Jews have to give up their property, observe curfew, and wear a yellow star of David on their clothing. The hope that they will only be held in the ghettos until the end of the war dies with the Nazi order for deportation. The Jews of Sighet are loaded onto cattle wagons. There is inadequate food and water, and they are so crowded that they have to take turns sitting and cannot lie down at all. During the transport a villager named Madame Schächter begins to scream about visions of fires while her little son tries to comfort her. Later the other prisoners beat her to silence her.

The convoy finally stops at Auschwitz. The prisoners are told that they have arrived at a work camp, where families can stay together in relatively good conditions. From the windows of the cattle car, the prisoners see flames from a chimney silhouetted against the night sky. They have arrived at Birkenau, reception center for Auschwitz.

Literary Elements
Motif

Night: As a young boy, Eliezer looks forward to his time of prayer at dusk and later his nightly study of the cabbala with Moché the Beadle. Once the German occupation dominates life in Sighet, night becomes the backdrop for terror, a "long dark night of the soul." The news of deportation comes at midnight. In dread of the deportation, Wiesel remembers, "Night. No one prayed, so that the night would pass quickly. The stars were only sparks of the fire which devoured us." The transportation to Auschwitz in a cattle car is "[a]n endless night." It is against the night sky that the prisoners first see the flames of Auschwitz.

Eyes: Wiesel uses eyes to characterize people.
- Moché the Beadle has "dreaming eyes" when he is first described. Though he survives a massacre, the "joy in his eyes" is gone; he closes them "as though to escape time" and walks through the streets with his eyes downcast. His liveliness is replaced with suffering and shame—shame over his Cassandra-like failure to make the Jews of Sighet understand their plight.
- Madame Schächter is described as a woman with "burning eyes," her hysteria a reflection of the world's chaos, but after she is beaten into silence her gaze becomes "bewildered" and she appears to no longer even see her fellow prisoners.

Themes

Emotional Death: The absence of feeling dominates this section of the book.
- Moché the Beadle explains to Eliezer that his mission is to tell the story of his death.
- After the first evacuation, the ghetto is described as "[a]n open tomb, a dwelling place in which no one genuinely dwells."
- Madame Schächter, like Moché the Beadle, is a shadow of one who is fully alive— "dumb . . . absent."

Struggle to maintain faith: Eliezer's faith flourishes despite his father's lack of enthusiasm. The answer Moché the Beadle gives Eliezer about the point of prayer—to ask God for the strength to ask the right questions—introduces the struggle of the practice of faith. As the book progresses, Eliezer will see this theme as more and more central to his experience.

In hindsight, the narrator also comments on what he perceives to be his father's naiveté regarding the harmlessness of wearing the star of David—symbol for the faith that made Jews a target for Nazi extermination.

Dignity in the face of inhuman cruelty: The continued practice of religious observances despite the confinement into ghettos and the threat of deportation helps maintain dignity by providing some sense of normalcy and a link with the community's past.

Self-preservation versus family commitment: Madame Schächter's son's silence during her beating illustrates how the instinct for self-preservation can blot out family love and commitment.

Foreshadowing

- Moché the Beadle sings of the Exile of Providence, an allusion to the expulsion of the Jews from their homeland of Judah in the sixth century B.C. Eliezer wept over the destruction of the Temple, which refers to the temple of Solomon destroyed by Nebuchadnezzar during the Babylonian occupation of Jerusalem.
- Madame Schächter's screams about fires foreshadow the horrors of the crematory.

Part II: Birkenau-Auschwitz to Buna

Plot Synopsis

At Birkenau, the guards separate the prisoners. Eliezer and his father are sent with the men and boys. His mother and sisters go with the women and girls. Eliezer will never see his mother or sister Tzipora again. He is determined to remain with his father. By lying about his age, Eliezer manages to stay with the adult men. As guards march the men to barracks, Eliezer sees a load of children being taken to a flaming pit. His father begins to pray, but Eliezer realizes that the sight of this burning ditch has destroyed his faith in God.

At the barracks guards strip and shave the prisoners and make them run naked to showers where they are "disinfected" with gasoline. The prisoners are issued ragged and ill-fitting prison clothes and marched from Birkenau to Auschwitz. All along they are beaten by other prisoners.

A young Polish man in charge of Eliezer's barracks tells the prisoners that they have escaped "selection" to the crematory and encourages them to keep together and remain faithful. The next day veteran prisoners engrave (tattoo) numbers on the arms of the new prisoners, Eliezer included. For several days Eliezer proudly refuses to eat the thin soup given to prisoners, but he finally gives in to his hunger. After several weeks, the Germans march the prisoners to another camp, Buna.

There the prisoners are examined by doctors and selected for work assignments. Eliezer and his father go to work in a warehouse counting small pieces of electrical equipment, a relatively safe and easy job. A young French girl comforts Eliezer after he is beaten at random by the *Kapo,* or foreman, Idek. In a narrative flash forward to a time after the war has ended, Wiesel recognizes the woman in the Paris subway and they reminisce about the event. At Buna, Eliezer receives another severe beating after he accidentally sees Idek with a female prisoner.

During an air raid, the prisoners gain some measure of confidence that the war may soon be over and the Germans defeated. Eliezer, who had been separated from his father during the raid, joyfully sees his father again. Ironically, the only person killed during the raid is a prisoner who moved out into the open to try to steal some soup.

As the Russian front moves toward Buna, the Nazis execute prisoners for conspiring to commit sabotage. The hanging of a boy for alleged involvement with a saboteur concludes this section of *Night*. For Eliezer, the child hanging on the scaffold is God.

Literary Elements

Motif

Night: The imagery of night is extended by the description of the camp experiences as nightmares from which Eliezer never awoke and "nocturnal silence which deprived [him], for all eternity, of the desire to live."

Eyes: For the narrator, eyes remain a reliable indicator of spiritual states.

- His father's "eyes had grown dim" in the camp.
- The officer who showed kindness to the children had a smile "in his gray-blue eyes."
- The young French girl who cared for Eliezer after he was beaten was recognized by Wiesel years later on the Metro because of her "dreamy eyes."
- Franek, the foreman, who extorts a gold-crowned tooth from Eliezer, had eyes that "gleamed with desire."
- After the air raid, the prisoners had hope in their eyes.

Themes

Dignity in the face of inhuman cruelty: Through the kindness of a fellow prisoner, Eliezer and his father stay together and avoid selection by lying about their ages. This kindness is juxtaposed with the outrage of a second prisoner who curses them for their ignorance about Auschwitz. Small joys and kindnesses shield Eliezer from the dehumanizing effect of terror: the genuine joy of greeting familiar faces, the "human words" of the Pole in charge of the block at Auschwitz, Eliezer's effort to protect his relative from

the truth about his family, and the French girl's soothing words to Eliezer after he is beaten.

Self-preservation versus family commitment: In the course of his first night, overwhelmed to the point of feeling nothing, Wiesel explains that "[t]he instincts of self-preservation, of self-defense, of pride, had all deserted us." Concern for self does return, however, and twice prevents Eliezer from helping his father while his father is being beaten, a failure of commitment for which the boy is deeply ashamed. Wiesel also recounts the story of a *pipel* who beat his own father for failure to make his bed properly.

Emotional death: The presence of physical death is pervasive: the crematory, the ditches full of the bodies of children, and the selection. As a result, the living say the Kaddish for themselves, and the food tastes like corpses. Though Eliezer and his father escape physical death, Eliezer is "consumed in the flames" and is only the shell of the person he had been in Sighet. The situation is further exacerbated by the replacement of his name with a number. Ironically, the prisoners no longer fear the physical death that an air raid might bring; it frightens the Kapo, however, who maintains a position of privilege even though he, too, is a prisoner.

Struggle to maintain faith:

- Older prisoners beg the younger ones not to lose faith. While his father prays, Eliezer questions God; despite this questioning attitude, he also recites the Kaddish.
- That first night in the camp, the atrocities Eliezer witnesses kills his faith just as the children are killed.
- The kind words of the young Polish prisoner encourage faith. The prisoners cling to Hasidic songs and numerology to survive the ordeal. Some see the persecution as a test from God. Eliezer feels like Job—tested by God—but he ultimately ceases to pray.

- Eliezer assigns God's existence to the young *pipel* hanging on the gallows, indicating that the Nazis are murdering his faith.

- There is a sad irony in Eliezer's loss of faith—a faith that at one time so inspired him that he wished to be a rabbi and that is responsible for his imprisonment.

Part III: Buna to Buchenwald

Plot Synopsis

Prisoners celebrate Rosh Hashanah, the Jewish New Year, and Eliezer condemns the God he once worshiped. No longer faithful, Eliezer does not fast for Yom Kippur, the Day of Atonement, though this is partly because his father insists he eat to maintain his strength.

As the war front moves closer to Buna, the Germans again begin selecting prisoners to die in the crematoria. The head of the prisoners encourages the men to appear strong enough for work so that they won't be chosen, and Eliezer and his father escape selection once again.

Following an operation on his infected foot, Eliezer is in the camp hospital. Word that the front continues to advance toward Buna starts rumors of a camp evacuation. Afraid that the Germans will kill all the invalids unable to evacuate, Eliezer and his father decide to leave the hospital before Eliezer has fully recovered from his operation. Later he learns that the hospital patients left behind were liberated by Russians two days after the evacuation.

At nightfall, the prisoners begin the march out of Buna. The German soldiers force them to run through the snow, and shoot those who slow down. Prisoners who collapse are crushed under the feet of those behind them. After running all night, the prisoners rest. Eliezer and his father struggle to find a place inside an abandoned brick factory and to resist the temptation to sleep for fear of freezing to death. With nightfall the marching resumes, now much more slowly. The prisoners and guards finally reach their destination, the camp at Gleiwitz. The barracks are so crowded that men suffocate under the weight of other bodies. Eliezer finds his father still alive. In the pitch dark, Eliezar hears Juliek playing Beethoven on his violin; in the morning, Juliek is dead.

After three days in the barracks without food or water, the prisoners are transported to Buchenwald. During the journey, many die and their corpses are thrown out into the snow when the train stops. Survivors kill each other for scraps of bread. Of the hundred men originally in the cattle wagon which held Eliezer and his father, only twelve survive. Eliezer and his father are among them.

At Buchenwald Eliezer's father becomes ill with dysentery. Eliezer trades his bread ration with a prisoner in his father's bunk to stay near him. The camp doctors refuse to help, and other prisoners torment the dying man. Eliezer is enraged but helpless. At one point, Eliezer's father cries out in pain and an SS officer deals a violent blow to his head. The next morning, when Eliezer awakens, his father is gone and another invalid is in his place.

In the spring of 1945, as the front draws near, the Germans begin to evacuate and kill the remaining prisoners. The prisoners resist and the resistance leads to a revolt. The Germans flee, and U.S. troops enter the camp the same day. Sick with food poisoning after liberation, Eliezer is hospitalized for two weeks. When he recovers, the eyes that look back at him from the face in the hospital mirror are the eyes of a corpse.

Literary Elements

Motif

Night: The winter nights are long and cold; as the tide of war turns against Germany, the prisoners are moved during these cold nights. Each night of running means more dead.

- It is night when Eliezer is almost strangled by a fellow passenger on the train.
- One evening the "death rattle" of all the prisoners rises up from the trains.
- At night the train arrives in Buchenwald.
- At dusk the first Americans arrive to liberate the camp.

Eyes:

- The decline of Eliezer's father can be traced through his eyes, at first "tired" and "veiled with despair." Eliezer describes his father's eyes as "petrified" while they are seeking shelter from the cold in the brick factory. Once back on the train, it is only the slight movement of Eliezer's father's eyes that indicates he is alive and saves him from being thrown from the train. The "thankfulness in his eyes" for Eliezer's kindness gives way to a "visionary gaze," and shortly thereafter he dies.
- Akiba Drumer accepts death even before he is "selected," and his eyes are "glazed" and blank.
- An old man with a gleam in his eyes stealthily snatches a piece of bread.
- The final comment of the narrator is that he has the eyes of a corpse. This conclusion is foreshadowed early in the memoir: "Night. No one prayed, so that the night would pass quickly. The stars were only sparks of the fire which devoured us. Should that fire die out one day, there would be nothing left in the sky but dead stars, dead eyes." The fire is symbolic of the fires of the crematory, which finally did die out, but left those still living emotionally dead.

Themes

Struggle to maintain faith:

- This section opens with the celebration of Rosh Hashanah, and the narrator's rejection of faith and angry questions directed to God. Yet the asking of questions is reminiscent of the lesson of Moché the Beadle: "Man raises himself toward God by the questions he asks Him."
- The struggle to maintain faith and the eventual loss of it leaves a void in Eliezer's heart, results in Akiba Drumer's loss of hope, and, ironically, causes the Hungarian hospital patient with the "dead eyes" to put more faith in Hitler than in God.
- Despite his loss of faith, Eliezer prays to God for the strength to not abandon his father.

Dignity in the face of inhuman cruelty:

- The celebration of Rosh Hashanah and the wishing of Happy New Year to one another are expressions of hope (when there is little rational reason to hope) and tradition.
- The head of the block insists before evacuation that the men clean the block for the liberating army: "So that they'll realize there were men living here and not pigs."
- There is dignity in Eliezer's kindness to Rabbi Eliahou, whose son, Eliezer realizes, has abandoned his father.

Self-preservation versus family commitment:

This conflict is most keenly presented in the relationships between sons and fathers.

- On the transport to Buchenwald, a son named Meir beats his father to death for a scrap of bread.
- Rabbi Eliahou's son deserts his father to free himself of the burden.
- Eliezer prays to have the strength to resist the urge to abandon his father. He encourages his father and avoids separation from him, but he also admits being more concerned about himself than about his father after the air raid in Buchenwald and when his father is being beaten.
- The head of the block in Buchenwald explains to Eliezer, "Here, every man has to fight for himself and not think of anyone else. Even of his father."

Emotional Death: Physical death no longer frightens the prisoners, indicating emotional indifference to life. On the death march from Buna, Eliezer finds him-

Plot Synopsis and Literary Elements (cont.)

self fascinated by the idea of death, of release from his body. Those freezing in the night on the march do not even ask for help. The author explains, "[y]ou died because you had to die. There was no fuss." The sight of the crematory at Buchenwald does not faze the prisoners.

The emotional death Eliezer suffers is the result of the loss of his religious faith as well as of a sense of purpose. The final image of his own mirrored face, a corpse staring back at him, reflects an emotional death that his physical survival could not prevent.

Reader's Log: Model

Reading actively

In your reader's log you record your ideas, questions, comments, interpretations, guesses, predictions, reflections, challenges—any responses you have to the books you are reading.

Keep your reader's log with you while you are reading. You can stop at any time to write. You may want to pause several times during your reading time to capture your thoughts while they are fresh in your mind, or you may want to read without interruption and write when you come to a stopping point such as the end of a chapter or the end of the book.

Each entry you make in your reader's log should include the date, the title of the book you are reading, and the pages you have read since your last entry (pages ____ to ____).

Example

> Sept. 21
>
> <u>Fahrenheit 451</u>
>
> pages 3 to 68
>
> This book reminds me a lot of another book we read in class last year, <u>1984</u> by George Orwell. They're both books about the future—<u>1984</u> was written in the 1940s so it was the future then—a bad future where the government is very repressive and you can be arrested for what you think, say, or read. They're also both about a man and a woman who try to go against the system together. <u>Fahrenheit 451</u> is supposed to be about book censorship, but I don't think it's just about that—I think it's also about people losing their brain power by watching TV all the time and not thinking for themselves. <u>1984</u> did not have a very happy ending, and I have a feeling this book isn't going to either.

Exchanging ideas

Exchange reader's logs with a classmate and respond in writing to each other's most recent entries. (Your entries can be about the same book or different ones.) You might ask a question, make a comment, give your own opinion, recommend another book— in other words, discuss anything that's relevant to what you are reading.

Or: Ask your teacher, a family member, or a friend to read your most recent entries and write a reply to you in your reader's log.

Or: With your teacher's guidance, find an online pen pal in another town, state, or country and have a continuing book dialogue by e-mail.

Reader's Log: Starters

When I started reading this book, I thought . . .

I changed my mind about . . . because . . .

My favorite part of the book was . . .

My favorite character was . . . because . . .

I was surprised when . . .

I predict that . . .

I liked the way the writer . . .

I didn't like . . . because . . .

This book reminded me of . . .

I would (wouldn't) recommend this book to a friend because . . .

This book made me feel . . .

This book made me think . . .

This book made me realize . . .

While I was reading I pictured . . . (Draw or write your response.)

The most important thing about this book is . . .

If I were (name of character), I would (wouldn't) have . . .

What happened in this book was very realistic (unrealistic) because . . .

My least favorite character was . . . because . . .

I admire (name of character) for . . .

One thing I've noticed about the author's style is . . .

If I could be any character in this book, I would be . . . because . . .

I agree (disagree) with the writer about . . .

I think the title is a good (strange/misleading) choice because . . .

A better title for this book would be . . . because . . .

In my opinion, the most important word (sentence/paragraph) in this book is . . . because . . .

(Name of character) reminds me of myself because . . .

(Name of character) reminds me of somebody I know because . . .

If I could talk to (name of character), I would say . . .

When I finished this book, I still wondered . . .

This book was similar to (different from) other books I've read because it . . .

This book was similar to (different from) other books by this writer because it . . .

I think the main thing the writer was trying to say was . . .

This book was better (worse) than the movie version because . . .

(Event in book) reminded me of (something that happened to me) when . . .

Double-Entry Journal: Models

Responding to the text Draw a line down the middle of a page in your reader's log. On the left side, copy a meaningful passage from the book you're reading—perhaps a bit of dialogue, a description, or a character's thought. (Be sure to note the number of the page you copied it from—you or somebody else may want to find it later.) On the right side, write your response to the quotation. Why did you choose it? Did it puzzle you? confuse you? strike a chord? What does it mean to you?

Example

Quotation	Response
"It is a truth universally acknowledged, that a single man in possession of a good fortune must be in want of a wife." (page 1)	This is the first sentence of the book. When I first read it I thought the writer was serious—it seemed like something people might have believed when it was written. Soon I realized she was making fun of that attitude. I saw the movie <u>Pride and Prejudice</u>, but it didn't have a lot of funny parts, so I didn't expect the book to be funny at all. It is though, but not in an obvious way.

Creating a dialogue journal Draw a line down the middle of a page in your reader's log. On the left side, comment on the book you're reading—the plot so far, your opinion of the characters, or specifics about the style in which the book is written. On the right side of the page, your teacher or a classmate will provide a response to your comments. Together you create an ongoing dialogue about the novel as you are reading it.

Example

Your Comment	Response
The Bennet girls really seem incredibly silly. They seem to care only about getting married to someone rich or going to balls. That is all their parents discuss, too. The one who isn't like that, Mary, isn't realistic either, though. And why doesn't anyone work?!	I wasn't really bothered by their discussion of marriage and balls. I expected it because I saw the movie <u>Emma</u>, and it was like this, too. What I don't understand is why the parents call each other "Mr." and "Mrs."—everything is so formal. I don't think women of that class were supposed to work back then. And people never <u>really</u> work on TV shows or in the movies or in other books, do they?

Name _____ Date _____

Group Discussion Log

Group members

....

....

....

....

....

Book discussed

Title: ....

Author: ....

Pages _____ to _____

Three interesting things said by members of the group

....

....

....

....

....

....

What we did well today as a group

....

....

....

....

What we could improve

....

....

....

....

Our next discussion will be on _____. We will discuss pages _____ to _____.

- **Vocabulary Words** are preceded by an asterisk (*) and appear in the Vocabulary Worksheets.
- Words are listed in their order of appearance.
- The definition and the part of speech are based on the way the word is used in the chapter. For other uses of the word, check a dictionary.

Parts I and II: Sighet to Buna

Hasidic: of a Jewish sect of mystics that originated in Poland in the eighteenth century, which stresses joyful worship of a God believed to be present in everything

synagogue *n.:* a building used by Jewish people for religious study and worship

cabbala *n.:* an occult Jewish philosophy based on a mystical interpretation of the Scriptures

Talmud: a book of detailed expositions and interpretations of Hebrew scriptures; the writings that make up Jewish law

the destruction of the Temple: King Nebuchadnezzar of Babylon captured the Jewish city of Jerusalem and destroyed its Temple in 587 B.C.

Maimonides: a twelfth-century Spanish rabbi and one of the most revered of Jewish philosophers

Gestapo: the secret police force of the German Nazis

lorries *n.:* trucks

rabbi *n.:* a scholar and teacher of Jewish law; the spiritual leader of a Jewish congregation

Zionism: formerly, a movement for reestablishment of a Jewish state; now, a movement supporting the Jewish state of Israel

*emigration *n.:* the act of leaving one country or region to settle in another

*abstraction *n.:* a generality; an idea or thought separated from concrete reality

billeted *v.:* lodged; used to refer to temporary lodging of military personnel in private homes or other private buildings

Passover: a Jewish holiday celebrating the deliverance of the Hebrews from slavery in Egypt

treatise *n.:* a formal article or book on a particular subject

*expounding *v.:* stating in detail; explaining

premonition *n.:* a feeling that something is about to happen, especially something bad

*edict *n.:* an official public proclamation or order issued by an authority, such as a governmental or military authority

phylacteries *n.:* small cases holding copies of passages from Scripture worn on the forehead and left arm during weekday morning prayers.

truncheons *n.:* short, thick cudgels or clubs

the captivity of Babylon: the period from 597 B.C. to 538 B.C., during which Jerusalem was conquered by King Nebuchadnezzar and the Jewish people were sent into captivity in Babylon

Spanish Inquisition: the brutal persecution (primarily in the fifteenth and sixteenth centuries) of those accused of heresy, including non-Christians such as Jews, by the Catholic Church

compatriots *n.:* fellow countrymen

Boche: a derogatory name for a German, especially a German soldier in World War I

guerrillas *n.:* small groups of soldiers, often volunteers, who make surprise attacks and raids behind enemy lines

*expulsion *n.:* a driving out, especially by force

*pillage *v.:* to loot; to rob of property

*constraint *n.:* restriction, especially of feelings and behaviors

hermetically *adv.:* in an airtight way

barometer *n.:* literally, an instrument for measuring atmospheric pressure; an indicator of change

SS: abbreviation of *Schutzstaffel;* a military-style unit of the Nazi party that acted as a special police force

*incite *v.:* to urge to act; to provoke

*unremittingly *adv.:* constantly; without interruption

*nocturnal *adj.:* of or happening during the night

*bestial *adj.:* like a beast; cruel and savage

*lucidity *n.:* clearheadedness; clarity; rational understanding

*oblivion *n.:* state of being completely forgotten

*harangued *v.:* scolded, especially in a noisy and bullying way

Kapos: Nazi concentration camp prisoners who were given special privileges in return for supervising other prisoners on work crews. Kapos were often common criminals and were notorious for their brutality toward fellow inmates.

*compulsory *adj.:* required; that which must be done

*wizened *adj.:* shriveled; dried up

*base *adj.:* ignoble; inferior; undignified

blandishments *n.:* flattering remarks that are meant to be persuasive

*sanctity *n.:* holiness; sacredness

numerology *n.:* an occult system, built around numbers, of foretelling the future or exploring the unknown

*reprieve *n.:* a postponement of punishment; a temporary relief

Aryan: a term used by the Nazis to mean a Caucasian person of non-Jewish lineage

*raucous *adj.:* loud and rough-sounding; hoarse

Part III: Buna to Buchenwald

Rosh Hashanah: the Jewish New Year, the spiritual new year whose observances include special prayers and religious rituals

*functionaries *n.:* people who perform certain expected duties, especially official functions

benediction *n.:* formal blessing; act of calling upon God during a religious service

*implored *v.:* begged; pleaded sincerely

*lamentation *n.:* an expression of grief or sadness

*countenance *n.:* face or features of the face

Yom Kippur: the holiest day in the Jewish calendar, the Day of Atonement, a day of fasting and prayer for forgiveness

Achtung: German for "attention"

*interminable *adj.:* endless or seeming to be endless

*emaciated *adj.:* abnormally thin, especially due to starvation or disease

*meager *adj.:* of small quantity; not adequate

crucible *n.:* container or vessel made of a substance that can withstand extreme heat; a severe trial or test

*inconsiderable *adj.:* unimportant; small

sage *n.:* a person who is very wise, especially one whose great wisdom is the result of age and experience

Calvary: literally, the place near Jerusalem where Jesus was crucified; here, used metaphorically to mean an experience of intense agony or grief

*derision *n.:* scorn; ridicule

dysentery *n.:* intestinal inflammation causing abdominal pain and severe diarrhea; often fatal if left untreated in the very young or old, or in those who are weakened by hunger or other disease

Red Army: the regular army of the former Soviet Union

*annihilate *v.:* destroy completely; exterminate

*summarily *adv.:* promptly and without formality

mountebanks *n.:* fakes; charlatans or tricksters

knell *n.:* the sound of a bell, especially of a bell rung slowly at a funeral; often used metaphorically to mean a bad omen

*indeterminate *adj.:* indefinite; vague; subtle

*stupefied *adj.:* stunned; amazed

*privations *n.:* hardships; lack of necessities of everyday life

*encumbrance *n.:* burden; obstacle

*semblance *n.:* appearance; resemblance

*apathy *n.:* lack of interest or emotion; indifference

*vigilance *n.:* the state of watchfulness; alertness, especially to danger

*appeasing *v.:* satisfying; relieving

*inert *adj.:* motionless; lacking the ability to move or act

visionary *adj.:* having the nature of a vision; unreal

First Thoughts

1. In your opinion, why might the Jews of Sighet refuse to believe the stories of the horrors committed by the Nazis—even when told by one who witnessed them?

Shaping Interpretations

2. The narrator mentions the Exile of Providence and the destruction of the Temple at the beginning of his account. These **allude** to (refer to) the expulsion of the Jews from their homeland of Judah in the sixth century B.C. Explain how this allusion **foreshadows** events in this section of *Night*.

3. Describe the relationship between Eliezer and his father, using details from the book to support your description.

4. A **motif** is a word, character, object, image, metaphor, or idea that recurs throughout a literary work. Wiesel uses eyes as a motif in order to characterize those around him. Compare and contrast the description of Moché the Beadle before and after his deportation. Explain how the description of his eyes reveals his personality.

5. Explain how night is also a significant **motif** in this account. Cite specific details from the book to support your explanation.

6. **"The yellow star? Oh well, what of it? You don't die of it. . . ."**
(Poor Father! Of what then did you die?)
Ironic statements can illustrate the difference between appearance and reality. Explain how this passage from the text is sadly ironic.

7. Describe one example of **foreshadowing** that suggests what Eliezer and the other prisoners will discover at Birkenau.

Extending the Text

8. Viktor E. Frankl, psychiatrist and concentration camp survivor, wrote about his concentration camp experience, "An abnormal reaction to an abnormal situation is normal behavior." Tell why you agree or disagree with this statement. What in Eliezer's experience of deportation to Birkenau-Auschwitz seems to prove this statement true?

Challenging the Text

9. Wiesel decided to wait a decade before attempting to express his experience in words. Tell why you think this was, or was not, a good decision. What may have been gained or lost during that silent decade?

Writing Opportunity

From what you have read so far, why is *Night* an appropriate title for Eliezer's story?

Reading Strategies: Part I

Night

Understanding a Motif

A **motif** in literature is a word, character, object, image, metaphor, or idea that recurs and usually bears an important relationship to the theme of a work.

A. The *connotations* of a word—the meanings, associations, or emotions that a word suggests—often enable it to act as a motif.

What are some connotations of the word *night?*

....

....

....

B. Locate three examples of the word *night* in the text. Identify the events which occur around the use of the word and tell what the word connotes in its context.

Example

Quotation	Event	Connotation
". . . at night I ran to the synagogue . . ."	At night he prays and later studies with Moché the Beadle	Night as a time of mystery and the mystical
1.		
2.		
3.		

FOLLOW-UP: How does the motif of *night* help develop the theme of emotional death?

Book Notes

Part I, *Night*

The Mystical Approach

The goal of most Western religions is to experience God. In Jewish mysticism, the cabbala is a means to this end. In this mystical tradition from the twelfth century, all souls are derived from a single soul, and every generation is coming closer to perfection. The cabbala teaches a believer how to become more receptive to divine forces and to trade material worries for spiritual growth.

Passed down by word of mouth for many centuries, this body of knowledge was expanded by each generation. The cabbalists prohibited study to those unprepared, and for this reason the cabbalists were often considered to be a secretive cult. Even now, there are few cabbalists outside of Israel. The entire cabbala is an extensive text, intellectually daunting, and not easily obtained.

The Zohar

The Zohar is the classic text of the cabbala. It consists of twenty-four volumes, and the knowledge and information in it are at least two thousand years old. It is a series of parables and discourses written in Aramaic, a language spoken in Biblical times. This book, believed to be magical, contains the answer to universal questions—Why do we exist? How was the universe created?—and explains the development of the human soul.

The Word PLACE

Ghetto

The Moors in Muslim Morocco started the practice of segregating Jews into ghettos—separate, usually walled-off areas—in 1280, and the practice spread throughout Europe, lasting well into the late nineteenth century. Jews could leave the ghetto during the day, but were forcibly returned to be locked in each night.

Zionism

History in a Nutshell:

In traditional Jewish texts, Mount Zion is the center of the world, the home to which the Jewish people would return when the Messiah came. For some Jews there was a radical break from this religious belief at the end of the nineteenth century.

No longer interested in waiting for the Messiah, the "Zionists," a religious-political organization headed by Theodor Herzl, decided to take matters into their own hands. The Zionists resolved to found their own entirely Jewish state, feeling that it was the only way Jews could survive in the modern world. They decided to relocate to what they viewed as their lost homeland—modern-day Israel.

INVESTIGATE · *Research the importance of geographical location to a world religion that interests you.*

Choices: Part I

Building Your Portfolio

ART

Occupied Territory

Create a map illustrating the setting for this portion of *Night*. Include Sighet, Birkenau, and Auschwitz. Try to include the forest of Galicia near Kolomaye as well. Color code countries around Hungary occupied by German forces and indicate the year that the German Army invaded each country.

CREATIVE WRITING/PERFORMANCE

Breaking News

Take the role of a television reporter breaking the news to viewers in the United States of the forced move of the Sighet Jewish community into ghettos. Write a script for your newscast based on *Night* and present your story to the class as if it were a live broadcast.

RETELLING/SUMMARIZING

The Flow of Events

Create with a partner a flowchart of events that clearly traces the reader's introduction to Sighet from before the German occupation to the arrival of the Jews of Sighet at Birkenau. Your chart should be large enough to be a classroom display. Add pictures (drawn or photocopied) to represent the events described in the boxes or circles of the flowchart.

LITERARY ANALYSIS

Book of Allusions

An **allusion** is a reference to someone or something that is known from history, literature, religion, or some other branch of culture. Wiesel uses allusions to set the tone of his account, provide foreshadowing, and to root his story in the context of the larger story of the Jewish people. Create a small booklet of these allusions: Exile of Providence, destruction of the Temple, Babylonian

captivity, Angel of Death, and the Spanish Inquisition. (You may add the word *holocaust* as well, even though it does not appear in the book) Your booklet should include a complete description of the original event or character to which Wiesel refers, a picture if possible or appropriate, and an explanation of how that allusion is significant in *Night*.

Consider This . . .

"There are a thousand and one gates leading into the orchard of mystical truth. Every human being has his own gate. We must never make the mistake of wanting to enter the orchard by any gate but our own. To do this is dangerous for the one who enters and also for those who are already there."

Describe the "orchard of mystical truth" in your own words.

Writing Follow-up: Personal Reflection ▬■

In a two- to four-paragraph response, explain your position on Moché the Beadle's philosophy as presented here. Include your interpretation of what he is saying, the elements of that philosophy with which you agree, and those with which you disagree.

Book Notes

Create an activity based on **Book Notes, Issue 1.** Here are two suggestions.

- Research Jewish mysticism and either Christian or Muslim mysticism. Be sure to cite your sources.
- Investigate what has happened to areas of European cities once set aside as Jewish ghettos.

First Thoughts

1. What in Elie Wiesel's account do you find most shocking?

Shaping Interpretations

2. The Kaddish is the Jewish prayer traditionally recited in memory of the dead. Explain how the prisoners' recitation of the prayer as they walk through Auschwitz conveys the **theme** of the struggle to maintain faith.

3. How is the **motif** of eyes used by Wiesel to characterize the personalities of the people in the camps?

4. How do the small joys and kindnesses that Eliezer describes illustrate the **theme** of human dignity in the face of inhuman cruelty?

READING CHECK

a. What is Eliezer's one thought after he and his father are separated from his mother and sisters?

b. What does Eliezer tell the guards is his age and occupation?

c. What kindness does Eliezer show to a relative he encounters in the camp?

d. Once in Buna, where do Eliezer and his father work?

e. Who shows kindness to Eliezer after he is beaten by a Kapo?

f. For what offense are two adults and a child hanged?

---

5. What comment does the behavior of fathers and sons in this portion of the book make on the **theme** of self-preservation versus family commitment?

6. What is **ironic** about the prisoners' reaction to the threat of death that the air raid brings?

7. How is the **motif** of night used to explain Eliezer's experiences in the camp?

8. Explain the transformation that has taken place in Eliezer's faith.

9. How do other prisoners reconcile what they are experiencing in the camp with their faith?

Connecting with the Text

10. What other works of literature, art, or music do you know that convey a theme found in *Night*? Explain why you find this treatment of the theme especially effective.

Extending the Text

11. The slogan over the entrance to Auschwitz, "Work is Liberty," is deeply ironic because it proclaims a positive value for a place of inhuman suffering and death. Why do you think people invent such slogans, and why do so many people respond to them enthusiastically?

Writing Opportunity

Present your response to this question in a paragraph or two.

Name _____ Date _____

Reading Strategies: Part II

Internal Conflict

The prisoners in *Night* face an overwhelming external conflict in the struggle against the Nazis. One of the most powerful elements of the book, however, is the internal conflict Wiesel documents—the struggle of faith within the narrator's heart and mind.

Fill in the top half of each oval with an event or a comment by Eliezer about the conflict he faces in his heart and mind. Then, in the bottom half of each oval, add your own comment about the conflict and what you think it reveals about Wiesel.

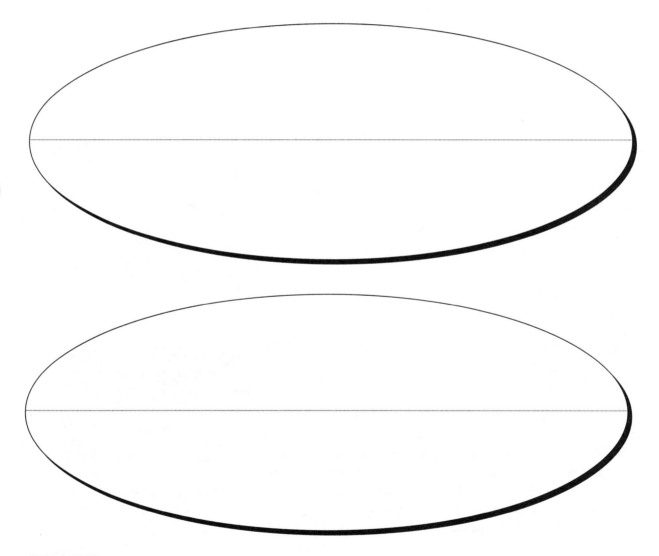

FOLLOW-UP

Explain how you think writing about an internal conflict may help to resolve it.

Book Notes

Part II, *Night*

The Word PLACE

Genocide

Geno from the Greek for "race" and *cide* from the Latin for "to cut down or kill" were not combined into one horrifying term until the Nazis' systematic murder of Jews and Romany people. There have been other genocides, both before the Holocaust (the massacre of the Armenians from 1915 to 1923) and after (the mass killing of Rwandan Tutsis in 1994). What makes genocides different from other atrocities is the attempt to murder an entire race or ethnic group.

HOLOCAUST

Holocaust comes from the Greek and literally means a "whole burnt offering." The practice of such offerings is recorded in the Bible and in Greek epics. As people attempted to make sense of the World War II genocide, they began to assign names to the catastrophe. The genocide was eventually given the label "Holocaust" to equate the Jews' sacrifice of their lives for their faith with the sacrifices at the Temple in Biblical times.

History in a Nutshell:

Persecution of the Romany People

The Nazis committed another, less well-known genocide. The Gypsies, or the Romany people, are a nomadic people believed to have originated on the Indian subcontinent and to have migrated into Europe in the Middle Ages. They are known for their distinctive Romany language and unique customs and culture which they have clung to throughout history. Romany people have often been victims of prejudice. Hitler and the Nazi Party considered them an inferior race and made their extermination, along with that of the Jews, part of their Final Solution of racial purification. The Romany people were interned in concentration camps such as Dachau as early as 1939, and by 1942 all the Romany were sent to concentration camps for extermination.

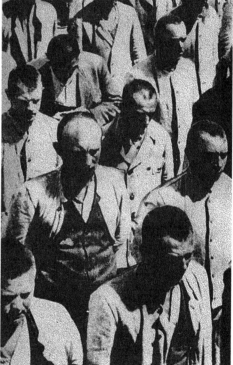

Although the estimate of the number of Romany people killed during World War II stands at a quarter of a million, the actual number remains unknown; thus this Nazi act of genocide is called "the forgotten Holocaust."

Choices: Part II

Building Your Portfolio

CREATIVE WRITING

Dear Diary

Journal writing and the experience of the Jewish people in World War II are forever linked to the memory of Anne Frank. The female experience is understandably absent in Wiesel's account. The reader of *Night* learns little of Eliezer's sisters Hilda and Béa. Based on what you can gather from the book, your imagination, and other sources, write a diary of the experiences of Hilda or Béa after arriving at Birkenau.

ART

Unspeakable Visions

Some survivors of the concentration camps have created drawings, paintings, and sculptures that express some aspects of their experiences. Use the library to find a reproduction of such a work. Write a brief report on the work and the person who created it. Add your own comments on what light the work throws on the events related in *Night*.

RESEARCH/PRESENTATION

Asking and Answering

There are many questions about the Holocaust that cannot be answered simply. *Night* answers some questions but raises others. Some questions that the book brings to mind *are* answerable, and answering them may help to clarify some of the larger issues. Create a book of questions and answers about the Holocaust. Here are some examples:

- Why are non-Jewish civilians in the camp as laborers?
- For whom are the prisoners working?
- Where were the female prisoners?
- Who became Kapos?
- Juliek is allowed to keep his violin. What possessions were others allowed to keep?

Share your questions and answers with the class.

GROUP PERFORMANCE

Round Table

Form a group of four to six students. One student will act as moderator. The others will act as diplomats from other countries and will research what was known about the camps during the war by European and non-European nations. Present the round-table discussion for the class. Two questions will be asked of the diplomats: What information did their countries have at the time, and what action did they take?

Provide source information to support your statements.

Consider This . . .

"Bite your lip, little brother. . . . Don't cry. Keep your anger and hatred for another day, for later on. The day will come, but not now. . . . Wait. Grit your teeth and wait. . . ."

What would you add to the French girl's advice to Eliezar after his beating by the Kapo?

Writing Follow-up:
Personal Reflection ——————————— ∎

Write a paragraph or two explaining how Eliezer interprets the French girl's advice and acts on it.

Book Notes

Create an activity based on **Book Notes, Issue 2.** Here are two suggestions.

- Research the Romany language.
- Investigate the effects of World War II on the people of India, Africa, or Australia.

First Thoughts

1. Eliezer seems to feel he did not respond as a son should to his dying father and that he did not respond appropriately after his father's death. What do you think of his behavior?

Shaping Interpretations

2. **"Man raises himself toward God by the questions he asks Him."** Moché was fond of repeating this statement to young Eliezer. How does this statement illuminate the narrator's struggle with faith at the celebration of Rosh Hashanah?

3. What are the results of the struggle of faith in Akiba Drumer?

4. The head of the block insists that the men clean the block before evacuating. How does this convey the **theme** of dignity in the face of inhuman cruelty?

5. During the movement of the prisoners from Buna, Eliezer notes several incidents in which sons betray their fathers. How do these events affect Eliezar? What insights do they provide into the **theme** of self-preservation versus family commitment?

6. Trace the decline of the health of Eliezer's father through the **motif** of his eyes.

7. What do you think the responses of the prisoners immediately after liberation reveal about them?

8. What comment does the conclusion of the book make on the **theme** of emotional death?

Extending the Text

9. The intense experience of World War II and the Holocaust brought out the worst and the best in many people. Based on what you know of history and what Wiesel writes in *Night,* what conclusions can you draw about human nature?

Challenging the Text

10. Wiesel devotes only a few lines to events after his liberation. Do you think this is an effective way to end the book? Why or why not? What else might Wiesel have done?

READING CHECK

a. Why does Eliezer not fast on Yom Kippur?

b. Why is Eliezer taken to the infirmary?

c. What happens to those patients who stay in the infirmary rather than beginning the march to Buchenwald?

d. What does Juliek do just before he dies?

e. Of the one hundred men in the train car with Eliezer and his father, how many arrive at Buchenwald?

f. Of what does Eliezer's father most likely die?

g. How are the SS finally driven from Buchenwald?

Writing Opportunity

Develop your response into a paragraph or two, and include an explanation of how and why Eliezer avoids being judgmental about the behavior of other sons toward their fathers.

Reading Strategies: Part III

Night

Theme

A **theme,** or insight into life offered by a work, is usually conveyed by the words and actions of the characters.

Review actions in this section of *Night* that exemplify dignity in the face of inhuman cruelty.

Inhuman Cruelty

Responding with Dignity

Abusive Kapos and being allowed only minimal food

On Rosh Hashanah . . .
....
....
....

Forbidden to play Beethoven, forced on a death march, freezing and crushed in barracks

Juliek . . .
....
....
....

The doctors will not attend Eliezer's father, the fellow prisoners beat him, no more food is given to him because he is dying.

YET

Eliezer . . .
....
....
....

FOLLOW-UP: In a paragraph or more, explain what the above examples of responding with dignity reveal about human nature. Include a statement of a theme about dignity in the face of inhuman cruelty.

Book Notes

Issue 3

Part III, *Night*

Rescuers: Raoul Wallenberg

"Righteous Gentiles" were non-Jews who attempted to rescue Jews from the Holocaust. Though the best known is Oskar Schindler, others also resisted the Nazis. One such man was Raoul Wallenberg, a Swedish businessman and diplomat. Traveling to Hungary, he risked his life by confronting Nazi officials and may have reduced the number of Hungarian Jews murdered by half.

After the war, he was imprisoned in a Russian prison camp. In 1981, the United States finally recognized him for his efforts, and he was made an honorary American citizen. His whereabouts remain unknown.

INVESTIGATE • *Who were some other rescuers during the Holocaust? What heroic actions did they take?*

TRIAL OF THE CENTURY

The first of the Nuremberg trials occurred directly after the end of World War II, from 1945 to 1946. Former Nazi leaders were tried as criminals, and many were either executed or imprisoned. There were twenty-one defendants, and the trials took over 216 court sessions, the proceedings of which were closely monitored by the rest of the world. New international laws resulted, concerning the civil rights of individuals during wartime and the responsibilities of soldiers following orders.

The Media Project
SURVIVORS OF THE SHOAH VISUAL HISTORY FOUNDATION

Because of the advancing age and frailty of Holocaust survivors, director Steven Spielberg began an urgent mission to preserve the oral history of the Holocaust. With the money he made from his film *Schindler's List,* Spielberg established the Survivors of the Shoah Visual History Foundation. This Los Angeles-based foundation aims to honor the past and hopes to protect the future. Using thousands of videographers and interviewers worldwide, the foundation has recorded and preserved over 50,000 testimonies and 100,000 hours of unedited video records of Jewish and non-Jewish Holocaust survivors, partisans, rescuers, war crimes tribunal staff members, and eyewitnesses to any part of the Holocaust story.

> **FOR YOUR READER'S LOG**
>
> Compare *Night* with one or two other testimonials of concentration camp survivors.

Choices: Part III

Building Your Portfolio

LITERARY ANALYSIS

Dark Night of the Soul

Night. No one prayed, so that the night would pass quickly. The stars were only sparks of the fire which devoured us. Should that fire die out one day, there would be nothing left in the sky but dead stars, dead eyes.

With a partner, analyze this statement made by the narrator prior to deportation from Sighet. Relate the statement to the events and experiences at the conclusion of Eliezer's time in the concentration camps. Explain the larger symbolic significance of *night, prayer, stars, fire,* and *dead stars, dead eyes.* Present your analysis to the class.

CREATIVE WRITING

Tribute in Verse

An **elegy** is a poem of mourning, lamenting and praising someone who has died or meditating on a sense of loss. Write an elegy for Eliezer's father, Juliek, Eliezer himself (who is emotionally dead), or any other person in the book. You may choose to make the speaker of your poem (the mourner) Eliezer, another prisoner, or yourself. Your elegy should be at least twelve lines in length.

ART

Mirror Image

Eliezer has not seen his own image since he left Sighet, and the reader is not given a detailed description of him. Based on pictures of those recently liberated or your impression of how he would look, draw the face that Eliezer sees looking back at him in the mirror. In whatever medium you choose, try to capture the tone of the concluding passage in the book.

Consider This . . .

My father's presence was the only thing that stopped me. . . . He was running at my side, out of breath, at the end of his strength, at his wit's end. I had no right to let myself die. What would he do without me? I was his only support.

If Eliezer's father had died sooner, do you think Eliezer would have still survived the camps?

Writing Follow-up:
Cause and Effect ━━━━━━━━━━━━━━■

Explain the cause-and-effect relationship between having a focus or purpose and survival. Present your ideas in a two- to four-paragraph response. Support your stance with examples from this text, other instances from history, or personal experience.

Book Notes

Create an activity based on **Book Notes, Issue 3.** Here are two suggestions:

- What happened to the notorious Dr. Mengele, a Nazi war criminal who was not tried at Nuremberg?
- Locate video footage or transcripts of the Nuremberg trials. Present selected excerpts for the class that give them a feel for the nature of the trials.

Name _____ Date _____

Book Review

MAJOR CHARACTERS

Use the chart below to keep track of the characters in this book. Each time
you come across a new character, write the character's name and the number
of the page on which the character first appears. Then, jot down a brief description. Add information about the characters as you read. Put a star next
to the name of each main character.

NAME OF CHARACTER	DESCRIPTION

FOLLOW-UP: A *dynamic character* changes in some important way as a result
of the story's action. In a paragraph, trace the transformation of one dynamic
character from the time the character is introduced through the conclusion of
the book.

Name _____ Date _____

Book Review (cont.)

Night

SETTING

Time ....

Most important place(s) ....

....

One effect of setting on plot, theme, or character ....

....

....

PLOT

List key events from the book.

- ....   - ....

- ....   - ....

- ....   - ....

Use your list to identify the plot elements below. Add other events as necessary.

Major conflict / problem ....

....

Turning point / climax ....

....

Resolution / denouement ....

....

MAJOR THEMES

- ....

- ....

- ....

Name _____ Date _____

Motif

Wiesel does not provide the reader with detailed physical descriptions of his narrator or others. He does, however, use the motif of eyes to reveal the thoughts and feelings of people throughout the book.

Identify the narrator's description of each individual's eyes and the behavior or personality of that individual.

Individual	Description of eyes	Behavior or personality
1. Moché the Beadle		
2. Madame Schächter		
3. the French girl		
4. Franek and the old man on the transport to Buchenwald		
5. Eliezer		

FOLLOW-UP:

- **What other character is described as having a dreamer's eyes? What are the narrator's feelings about individuals with dreamer's eyes in his life?**

Literary Elements Worksheet 2

Night

Theme

A literary work may have more than one theme, or insight into life. One of the themes of Elie Wiesel's *Night,* born out of his own experience with his father and observations of other sons and fathers, addresses self-preservation versus family commitment.

In the ovals, briefly describe interactions between sons and fathers that are part of *Night*.

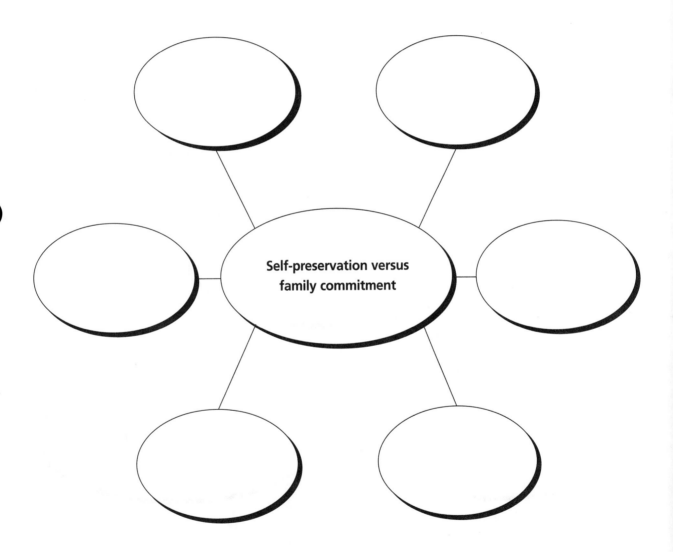

FOLLOW-UP: What does Elie Wiesel seem to be saying about the *balance* between self-preservation and commitment to family? What insight into life does *Night* offer on this topic?

Literary Elements Worksheet 3

Tone

Tone is the attitude of the writer toward his or her subject matter. In *Night,* Wiesel achieves a tone that is simultaneously personal and objective. He realizes that in most cases he needs only to present the facts; he does not try to interpret them.

Identify five events in *Night* that Wiesel presents without comment or interpretation.

FOLLOW-UP: Describe in your own words the overall effect of Wiesel's tone. How does his refusal to comment or interpret make you feel?

_____

_____

Vocabulary Worksheet 1 Parts I and II: Sighet to Buna

Night

A. Circle the letter of the word or phrase that most nearly defines the italicized word in each excerpt from *Night*.

1. My father was telling them anecdotes and *expounding* his own views on the situation.
- **a.** stating angrily
- **b.** drawing conclusions about
- **c.** making jokes about
- **d.** explaining in detail

2. In one ultimate moment of *lucidity* it seemed to me that we were damned souls wandering in the half-world. . . .
- **a.** tragedy
- **b.** clarity
- **c.** intelligence
- **d.** imaginativeness

3. These were the showers, a *compulsory* formality at the entrance to all these camps.
- **a.** required
- **b.** offensive
- **c.** unnecessary
- **d.** absurd

4. "He wants to find out whether we can dominate our *base* instincts and kill the Satan within us."
- **a.** ignoble
- **b.** unthinking
- **c.** significant
- **d.** boastful

5. Of course we had heard about the Fascists, but they were still just an *abstraction* to us.
- **a.** foreign military
- **b.** imaginary threat
- **c.** theoretical concept
- **d.** frightening thought

6. So many crazed men, so many cries, so much *bestial* brutality!
- **a.** needless
- **b.** savage
- **c.** methodical
- **d.** narrow-minded

7. Never shall I forget that *nocturnal* silence which deprived me, for all eternity, of the desire to live.
- **a.** harmful
- **b.** depressing
- **c.** endless
- **d.** nighttime

8. The baton moved *unremittingly,* sometimes to the right, sometimes to the left.
- **a.** constantly
- **b.** rhythmically
- **c.** heartlessly
- **d.** infrequently

9. The man looking for us was a bespectacled little fellow with a wrinkled, *wizened* face.
- **a.** scholarly
- **b.** gentle
- **c.** shriveled
- **d.** sneering

10. My father ran to right and left, exhausted, comforting friends, running to the Jewish Council to see if the *edict* had not been revoked in the meantime.
- **a.** false rumor
- **b.** guilty verdict
- **c.** official order
- **d.** forced deportation

Vocabulary Worksheet (cont.) Parts I and II: Sighet to Buna

Night

B. Read carefully the definition of each word. Then, write a sentence of your own using that word. If possible, include in your sentences clues to the meanings of the defined words.

11. constraint: *noun,* restriction, especially of feelings and behaviors

....

....

12. sanctity: *noun,* holiness; sacredness

....

....

13. reprieve: *noun,* postponement of punishment; temporary relief

....

....

14. incite: *verb,* to urge to act; to provoke

....

....

15. emigration: *noun,* the act of leaving one country or region to settle in another

....

....

C. Circle the letter of the pair of words that best expresses a relationship similar to that expressed in the original pair.

16. looters : pillage ::
  a. authors : write
  b. acrobats : compete
  c. librarians : read

17. expulsion : deportation ::
  a. education : observation
  b. superior : inferior
  c. investigation : examination

18. oblivion : forgetfulness ::
  a. bias : impartiality
  b. persistence : hesitation
  c. charity : kindness

19. harangued : hostility ::
  a. lamented : delight
  b. revered : admiration
  c. relieved : anguish

20. raucous : melodic ::
  a. musical : inharmonious
  b. rhythmic : beating
  c. boisterous : noisy

Vocabulary Worksheet 2 Part III: Buna to Buchenwald

Night

A. Circle the letter of the word or phrase that most nearly defines the italicized word in each excerpt from *Night*.

1. The race seemed *interminable.*
   - **a.** aimless
   - **b.** endless
   - **c.** inappropriate
   - **d.** illogical

2. A poor, *emaciated,* dried-up Jew questioned him avidly in a trembling voice.
   - **a.** extremely thin
   - **b.** hideously scarred
   - **c.** emotionally exhausted
   - **d.** utterly humiliated

3. We were given winter clothes—slightly thicker striped shirts. The veterans found in this a new source of *derision.*
   - **a.** rudeness
   - **b.** scorn
   - **c.** jealousy
   - **d.** bitterness

4. "All the invalids will be *summarily* killed," said the faceless one. "And sent to the crematory . . ."
   - **a.** systematically
   - **b.** secretly
   - **c.** promptly
   - **d.** individually

5. He sat up and looked round him, . . . *stupefied*—a bereaved stare.
   - **a.** amazed
   - **b.** frightened
   - **c.** ignorant
   - **d.** consoled

6. [H]e . . . had sought . . . to free himself from an *encumbrance* which could lessen his own chances of survival.
   - **a.** consequence
   - **b.** shortcoming
   - **c.** duty
   - **d.** burden

7. Man is . . . too humble and *inconsiderable* to seek to understand the mysterious ways of God.
   - **a.** insensitive
   - **b.** unwise
   - **c.** unimportant
   - **d.** insecure

8. Was it not dangerous to allow your *vigilance* to fail, even for a moment . . . ?
   - **a.** determination
   - **b.** watchfulness
   - **c.** strength
   - **d.** courage

9. At last, the morning star appeared in the gray sky. A trail of *indeterminate* light showed on the horizon.
   - **a.** subtle
   - **b.** deceptive
   - **c.** dull
   - **d.** distant

10. His body remained *inert.*
   - **a.** weak
   - **b.** thin
   - **c.** restless
   - **d.** motionless

Vocabulary Worksheet *(cont.)* Part III: Buna to Buchenwald

Night

B. Read carefully the definition of each word. Then, write a sentence of your own using that word. If possible, include in your sentences clues to the meanings of the defined words.

11. implored: *verb,* begged; pleaded sincerely

----

12. countenance: *noun,* face or features of the face

----

13. annihilate: *verb,* to destroy completely; to exterminate

----

14. meager: *adjective,* of small quantity; not adequate

----

15. semblance: *noun,* appearance; resemblance

----

16. apathy: *noun,* lack of interest or emotion; indifference

----

17. lamentation: *noun,* weeping; an expression of grief or sadness

----

18. privations: *noun,* hardships; lack of the necessities of everyday life

----

19. functionaries: *noun,* people who perform certain expected duties, especially official functions

----

20. appeasing: *verb,* satisfying; relieving

Book Projects

Writing About the Book

COMPARE AND CONTRAST

The Student Becomes the Teacher

Wiesel begins *Night* with Moché the Beadle. Compare and contrast Moché—his character, his deportation, and his altered personality upon his return to Sighet—with Eliezer at the outset of the book, during the camp internment, and upon liberation.
(Critical Writing)

SCRIPT WRITING

A Different Medium

Rework a particularly significant scene from the book into a scene for a play. Create additional dialogue to supplement the text, or convert narrative into dialogue. Include stage and acting directions.
(Creative Writing)

LITERARY ANALYSIS

Insight into Life

A **theme** is an insight into life offered by a text. Explore the theme of emotional death, self-preservation versus family commitment, or the struggle of faith as developed throughout *Night*. Begin your paper by stating what stance you believe that Wiesel takes on one of these issues, and use the text to support your opinion.
(Critical Writing)

COMPARISON

From *Night* to *Day*

Night does not have a sequel but it does have companion pieces: *Dawn* and *Day* (also called *The Accident*), which shed light on the life of survivors. Read either *Dawn* or *Day* and compare its characterization, themes, and motifs to those in *Night*.
(Critical Writing)

DEVELOPING THEME

Poetic Expression

Research poetry about the Holocaust or by survivors. Create an anthology of poems that connect with images, themes, or characters in *Night*. For each selection, write an explanation of the connection between the poem and *Night*. Your collection should include at least ten poems and ten explanations. Bind the collection, and create a cover that is appropriate for your anthology.
(Creative/Critical Response)

BIOGRAPHICAL RESEARCH

Testimony to Biography

Investigate Elie Wiesel's life after his liberation, and prepare a short biography about the Nobel Prize-winning author. Instead of simply reporting the facts of Wiesel's life, draw connections between the narrator of *Night* and the man who gave him his voice. Consider the insight into young Eliezer that is presented in *Night*, and research the author with the idea of discovering what became of the young survivor. Consider Wiesel's experiences in France, his struggle to become a writer, and his feelings about music and religion.
(Critical Writing)

Cross-Curricular Connections

Copyright © by Holt, Rinehart and Winston. All rights reserved.

HISTORY/SOCIAL STUDIES

Israel

When the Holocaust occurred, some European Jews considered emigration to Palestine, but decided not to leave home. A secret Jewish resistance force in Europe helped smuggle some Jews out of Europe to Palestine. Some of these people were turned away when they arrived. After the war, other nations cooperated to establish Israel as a permanent home for Jewish people. Research and write the history of the state of Israel from its founding through the 1967 Six-Day War. Present an outline of this history to the class.

ANALYZING THEME

Human Inhumanity

Research the Holocaust and one of these other examples of genocide or mass killing:

- the Armenian/Turkish conflict
- the Khmer Rouge in Cambodia
- the Rwandan civil war

Summarize the history of the Holocaust and the second atrocity that you choose. Compare them in terms of the relationship of the perpetrators and victims, the severity of the violence against the victims, the excuse for the aggression, the role of outsiders, and the outcome of the conflict.

GEOGRAPHY

Map of the Camps

Create a large map of Europe at the time of World War II. Locate the sites of at least six of the concentration and extermination camps. Briefly describe the history of each camp. Research when each camp opened and when it was liberated. Give the dates when extermination began and ended. List the number of people who died in each camp. Present your map and research to the class.

MUSIC/FOREIGN LANGUAGE

Sing Me a Song

"In the evening, . . . we would try to sing some of the Hasidic melodies. . . ." Locate examples of Hasidic melodies that might have been sung by Eliezer and the other prisoners. Either perform or play recordings of several selections for the class, and provide translations of the words.

HOME ECONOMICS

Passover Meal

The Jewish community of Sighet is celebrating Passover when the German army arrests their community leaders. Despite the fact that they are in a concentration camp with little food, the prisoners still celebrate Rosh Hashanah. Research the celebrations that are an integral part of the Jewish calendar and the food that is associated with them. Prepare several dishes that might be served on a Jewish holiday, such as Passover, and share them with the class. Explain to the class the significance of the dishes and the recipe and method of preparation.

PSYCHOLOGY

Man's Search for Meaning

Viktor E. Frankl, psychiatrist and concentration camp survivor, developed from his experiences a school of psychiatric thought—the school of logotherapy. Research Frankl; explain his conclusions about the motivating force of human life, and tell how his theory is a product of his experience in the camps. In your written or oral presentation of Frankl's school of thought, discuss how Eliezer's behavior in *Night* does or does not support Frankl's theory.

Multimedia and Internet Connections

NOTE: Check with your teacher about school policies on accessing Internet sites.

KEEPING THE MEMORY ALIVE

Building a Web Site

Many museums and Jewish organizations have created Web sites about the Holocaust. Plan one of your own. Describe the content you would create for your site. Include text, graphics, links to other sites, and contact information. Make a mock-up, on paper, of your site.

INTERVIEW: VIDEO

In Their Own Words

After he made the movie *Schindler's List,* Steven Spielberg founded the Survivors of the Shoah Visual History Foundation to videotape oral histories of the still-living survivors of the Holocaust. In a similar spirit of preserving the voices of those who experienced the Holocaust, create your own living history recording. Locate a camp survivor or someone who knew a survivor, a member of the armed forces who liberated the camps, or someone who lived in a German-occupied country and remembers the Jewish ghettos or deportation of Jews and non-Jews who is willing to participate in your project. Write a series of questions to encourage the person to tell his or her story and talk about the time period. Videotape a fifteen- to thirty-minute interview, including both your questions and the responses to them. *This is a sensitive subject area. Have your questions reviewed by your teacher for appropriateness, and provide the interviewee with a copy before the taping so that he or she will be more comfortable with the discussion.*

REVIEW: FILM

Moving Pictures

Watch a documentary or film based on the Holocaust. Write a review of the film that incorporates your impression of the production, and that relates the film to *Night.* Recommended films include *The Long Way Home* (NR), *Schindler's List* (R), *Life Is Beautiful* (PG-13), *The Lost Children of Berlin* (NR). *These films contain strong material. Consult with your teacher before viewing.*

MULTIMEDIA DESIGN: TELEVISION SPOT

In the Public Interest

Design and create a thirty-second public interest announcement to be shown on local television. Your spot should announce the beginning of a Holocaust Awareness program or a Prejudice Awareness program in your community. Design a symbol that will catch your audience's attention and convey the spirit of such a public awareness program. Animate your spot or use a series of still pictures or slides. Record a voiceover to accompany the images, and present the finished product to the class.

INTERNET RESEARCH

Other Victims

After reading *Night,* it is hard to imagine that anyone would subject another group to the hatred and persecution that led to the horrors of the Holocaust. Yet numerous groups have been the victims of organized hatred since the end of World War II. Use the Internet to learn about instances of persecution since the Holocaust. Begin your search at the Simon Wiesenthal Center. Identify several groups that have been victimized, and find out who the persecutors have been and what damage they have done. Also explore what is being done to combat hatred. Present your findings to the class using a computer-generated slide program or poster display charts.

Introducing the Connections

The **Connections** included in the HRW LIBRARY edition of *Night* reinforce the themes of the book and provide historical and social background. Succeeding pages offer **Making Meanings** questions to stimulate student response.

Selection	Summary, Connection to Book
The Mourner's Kaddish Traditional *prayer*	The Kaddish is a Jewish prayer traditionally recited by mourners during services after the death of a close relative, on the anniversary of the loved one's death, and in memorial services on certain holy days. Wiesel refers to the prayer in *Night* shortly after he and his father arrive in Auschwitz, and when thousands in the camp at Buna recite the Kaddish at the service marking the end of the Jewish year.
A Spring Morning Ida Fink *short story*	In this fictional account, a Jewish family prepares for a march toward death at the hands of SS soldiers. Recalling Wiesel's motif of *night,* there is no reprieve for Aron and his family from the day that is like "the blackest of black nights."
The Berlin-Bucharest Express Yaffa Eliach *personal narrative*	In this account based on an actual experience, a Jewish woman hears a remorseful German officer tell of his part in the murder of innocent Jews. The woman repeats the tale to her town's leaders, whose reaction recalls that of the citizens of Sighet to Moché's reports of Gestapo terror.
Maus Art Spiegelman *graphic novel excerpt*	This segment from the Pulitzer Prize-winning graphic novel is far from a "cartoon" about the Holocaust. It is the story of a son's discovery of his father's experience during the war. The classic fable technique of assigning human characteristics to animals allows the reader a level of detachment which may be necessary for examining such emotionally wrenching material and casts a new light on the issues introduced by Wiesel and other survivors.
The Treblinka Revolt Stanislaw Kohn *personal narrative*	Kohn relates the planning and execution of a revolt against the SS at the Treblinka concentration camp. The fact that so few of the rebels survived underlines the absolute horror of the camps described by Wiesel.
Mauthausen May 1945 / **My Black Messiah** Sonia Schreiber Weitz *personal narrative / poem*	In *Night,* Elie Wiesel describes the shock of seeing his own face after gaining his freedom. In this narrative and poem, the author describes the devastated expression on the face of one of her liberators.

Selection	Summary, Connection to Book
The Yellow Star S. B. Unsdorfer *personal narrative*	Wiesel's struggle in the camps encompasses both his fight for survival and his conflict with God. The author of this account, a Buchenwald prisoner, recounts the revival of his religious faith during the first days after the liberation.
The Trial of the Century Tom Post *news article*	This article describes the Nuremberg trials of Nazi leaders after World War II in a court set up by the Allies. The writer highlights the search for evidence against the Nazis and the courtroom showdown between the brilliant American prosecutor Robert Jackson and German field marshal Herman Göring.
But in the night Nelly Sachs *poem*	The heartache of Elie Wiesel and his concern for the fate of his family members during his imprisonment in the death camps are echoed in this poem of sorrow and longing for those who have died.
Babii Yar Yevgeny A. Yevtushenko *poem*	This poem was written to protest plans to build a sports stadium near Kiev, on the site of a Jewish massacre similar to the one described by Moché the Beadle in *Night*. Though he is not a Jew, the poet sees the site as a symbol of Jewish suffering and identifies with Jewish victims of persecution.
An Inner Freedom Viktor E. Frankl *personal narrative*	In this excerpt, the author draws on his experiences in a concentration camp to affirm the ability of men and women to rise above terrible conditions to attain inner freedom and preserve their dignity. As does Wiesel, Frankl realizes that a person's attitude toward his or her fate gives meaning to life.
A Cambodian Nightmare Alex Tizon *magazine article*	The cruelties described by Elie Wiesel in his memoir are echoed in this article about the Khmer Rouge takeover of Cambodia in the 1970s. The article highlights cultural beliefs and practices that have enabled Cambodian survivors of "the killing fields" to adjust to their new lives.
Why *Do* They Visit? John Aloysius Farrell *magazine article*	The writer explores reasons the United States Holocaust Memorial Museum, in Washington, D.C., receives so many visitors. Farrell suggests that people are led to ponder questions about Evil, Good, and God, the same questions that Elie Wiesel struggled with in Nazi death camps.
Nobel Peace Prize Acceptance Speech Elie Wiesel *speech*	In his speech accepting the 1986 Nobel Peace Prize, Wiesel affirms his dedication to preserving the memory of those who suffered in the Nazi death camps and his commitment to fighting injustice and persecution in all forms.

Exploring the Connections

Making Meanings

The Mourner's Kaddish

Connecting with the Book

What aspects of the Kaddish might have upset Eliezer during the religious service in the Buna concentration camp?

1. What thoughts and feelings expressed in the prayer make it appropriate for mourning?

2. In what ways is the prayer like a poem or the lyrics to a song?

READING CHECK

In addition to praising God, what does this prayer ask for?

A Spring Morning

Connecting with the Book

How is the use of the motif of "night" in this story similar to the manner in which it is used in *Night*?

1. What do you find admirable about Aron and his family?

2. List some images in the story that provide an ironic contrast with the family's situation. Explain the irony.

3. How do the flashbacks to earlier times in Aron's life affect the mood of the story?

4. How does the writer give the final scene a feeling that everything is happening in "slow motion"?

5. Compare and contrast the *tone* of this short story with that of Wiesel's *Night*.

READING CHECK

a. Why have the trucks come into Aron's town?

b. Why does Aron put his daughter down near the church?

c. What happens to Aron's daughter?

The Berlin-Bucharest Express

Connecting with the Book

Compare the reactions of the town leaders to Bronia's news of the Zhitomir killings with that of the people of Sighet to Moché the Beadle's story.

1. For which person in the story, Bronia or the German officer, do you feel more sympathy? Explain.

2. In what way do details about the **setting,** the time and place of the story, contribute to the story's impact?

3. As you read the officer's account, what questions came to mind?

4. Why do you think the German officer refuses to give Bronia a picture documenting the killings at Zhitomir?

5. Many of the Nazis on trial at Nuremberg defended their actions by saying that they were just following orders. Similarly, the German officer and his men committed murder under orders. What choices do you think the German officer had? Why do you think his conscience affected him after, rather than before, the killings?

READING CHECK

a. How did Bronia help Jews in Poland?

b. Why was the German secretary frightened?

c. Why was the German officer upset?

Exploring the Connections *(cont.)*

Making Meanings

Maus

Connecting with the Book

How does the **mood** of this selection compare with that of *Night?*

1. How does this comic-book style account of the Holocaust maintain the level of seriousness appropriate to the topic?

2. Why is the substitution of animals for people an effective means of telling about the atrocities of the Holocaust?

3. What do the first, sixth, and eleventh frames of this excerpt indicate about the narrative style of *Maus?*

4. **Mood** is the feeling created by a piece of writing, while the **tone** is the attitude a writer takes toward the subject of a work. What effect does the sentence structure and word choice of the "mice" narrating have upon the **mood** or **tone** of the account?

5. Throughout *Maus* Spiegelman portrays the Jewish characters as mice and the Germans as cats. How then do you interpret the significance of the shifting images in frames ten and eleven?

READING CHECK

a. Why was it better to be near the end of the soup line?

b. What did one of the prisoners claim to be the reason he did not belong at Auschwitz?

The Treblinka Revolt

Connecting with the Book

Compare and contrast Kohn's experience at Treblinka with Wiesel's account of imprisonment at Auschwitz and Buna.

1. Did the fact that there was a revolt at Treblinka surprise you? Why or why not?

2. How does the story about Max Brill **foreshadow** the events the memoir describes?

3. How do the descriptions of the atrocities of the concentration camp shape your response to the revolt?

READING CHECK

a. Why do the SS barracks bear the name Max Brill?

b. On the day of the revolt, why did the leaders decide to begin fighting an hour earlier than they had planned?

4. "The gas chambers will continue to function as long as a single Jew remains in the world." Why is this speech, which Kohn credits to SS *Untersturmführer* Franz, "significant"? What does it indicate about the situation the revolutionaries faced?

5. What effect do the details of plans for the revolt have on the pace of the narrative?

6. What clues does the text provide that the author takes some satisfaction in the rebellion, despite the number of prisoners who lost their lives?

Copyright © by Holt, Rinehart and Winston. All rights reserved.

Study Guide | **57**

Making Meanings

Connecting with the Book

Compare Weitz's description of the liberation of Mauthausen with Wiesel's description of the liberation of Buchenwald.

1. Of the images in this selection, which do you find the most striking or powerful?

2. How does the poem's imagery help you understand the soldier's reaction?

3. What message do you think the poet is trying to convey when she says that "we dare/To live, to hope, to smile"? *

4. Explain the significance of the title of the poem.

READING CHECK

a. Why did the writer and Edzia have difficulty climbing the hill to the camp at Mauthausen?

b. What happened at Mauthausen on May 4, 1945?

c. Why does the writer say that the innocence of the African American soldier was "forever slain"*?

The Yellow Star

Connecting with the Book

Explain how the recitation of the Kaddish and participation in a Jewish celebration have a different effect on Unsdorfer than on Wiesel.

1. What aspects of Unsdorfer's account surprised you? Why?

2. **Irony** is the contrast between what a reader expects to happen and what actually happens. Give an example of this type of **irony** from the narrative.

3. Compare Wiesel's and Unsdorfer's descriptions of the liberation of Buchenwald.

4. What is the common message of "The Yellow Star" and "I Believe"?

READING CHECK

a. Why were some Buchenwald prisoners leaving the camp with weapons?

b. Who were the *Mussulmänner?*

c. After the liberation, what did the narrator do to occupy his time in the camp?

d. What event at Buchenwald revived the narrator's religious faith?

*From "My Black Messiah" from "Mauthausen, May 1945" from *I Promised I Would Tell* by Sonia Schreiber Weitz, edited by Susan Belt Cogley. Copyright © 1993 by Sonia Schreiber Weitz. Reprinted by permission of ***Facing History and Ourselves.***

Making Meanings

Connecting with the Book

If Elie Wiesel had testified at the Nuremberg trials, what one incident might he have described as evidence of Nazi cruelty?

1. Based on the description in this article, would you have wanted to watch the Nuremberg trial if it had been shown on television?

2. Writers often **elaborate,** or develop their writing, with sensory details, facts and statistics, quotations, specific examples, and anecdotes. Name two types of elaboration the writer of this article uses, and give an example from the article of each type.

3. On what basis do you think the Nazi defendants claimed that they were not guilty?

4. What impact, if any, do you think the Nuremberg trials had on the moral behavior of governments throughout the world?

READING CHECK

a. What nations brought charges against the Nazi defendants?

b. What "new legal ground" did these nations break in the Nuremberg trial?

c. How successful was Robert Jackson in his prosecution of Nazi leaders?

Connecting with the Book

How might the idea that "humility makes you silent" explain why Wiesel did not write *Night* until ten years after liberation?

1. The poet speaks of dreamlike images. Which image in the poem do you find most striking or powerful?

2. **Tone** is the attitude the writer takes to his or her subject. Describe the tone of this poem.

3. Write one sentence that you think would fit *before* the first line of the poem.

4. Explain what is meant by "the death of the dead."

READING CHECK

a. What do the speaker's dreams allow her to do?

b. About what family members does the poet speak?

Making Meanings

Babii Yar

1. How does the fact that the poet is not Jewish affect the impact of the poem?

2. What is the effect of the poet's use of the first-person point of view?

3. An **allusion** is a reference to someone or something in history, literature, religion, or another branch of culture. How does the poet use allusions in "Babii Yar"?

4. Yevtushenko was reprimanded by Soviet authorities for writing "Babii Yar" twenty years after the 1941 massacre. What can you infer from this fact?

> **READING CHECK**
>
> **a.** With what young girl does the poem's speaker identify?
>
> **b.** How does the speaker describe the trees at Babii Yar?

An Inner Freedom

Connecting with the Book

Provide an example from *Night* that supports Frankl's assertion that humans are free to choose their attitude despite circumstances.

1. Do you agree that humans always have a choice of action? Why or why not?

2. A **first-person narrative** is an account of a writer's own experience. In what way is this personal narrative more effective than a scientific study?

3. How does this article address the **theme** of human dignity in the face of inhuman cruelty? Cite specific examples.

4. What do you think it means to be "worthy of your suffering"?

> **READING CHECK**
>
> **a.** According to Frankl, in what ways do humans have choices in the face of terrible circumstances?
>
> **b.** What did the condemned girl hear the tree say to her?

A Cambodian Nightmare

Connecting with the Book

Compare the attitudes of the Cambodians and the Jews toward their persecutors, based on the article and *Night*.

1. What words or phrases would describe your reactions to the account?

2. Why do Westerners know less about this story than about the Holocaust?

3. Why do you think Thailand at first refused to accept Cambodian refugees?

4. What might motivate survivors to talk and write about such a terrible experience as the Holocaust? Why might others choose to remain silent, as many survivors of the Khmer Rouge regime have done?

> **READING CHECK**
>
> **a.** What was the goal of the Khmer Rouge in Cambodia?
>
> **b.** What groups of people did the Khmer Rouge seek to eliminate?
>
> **c.** What cultural beliefs have helped Cambodians survive in their new homes?

Making Meanings

Connecting with the Book

In what way is reading *Night* in school similar to the museum experience? How is it different?

1. Does the information in the article make you want to visit the Holocaust museum? Why or why not?

2. What is the author's purpose for writing this article: to entertain, to persuade, or to inform? What techniques does the author use to achieve this purpose?

3. According to the article, why are contemporary U.S. citizens drawn to studying the Holocaust?

4. The writer says that "[i]n the face of both the hangman and the victim, we catch glimpses of ourselves." Do you agree or disagree with his statement? Explain.

READING CHECK

a. This article was written in September 1994. When did the Holocaust Museum open its doors?

b. Why had some Holocaust scholars been skeptical about the idea of a Holocaust museum?

c. What is the first image visitors to the museum see as they exit the elevator?

Nobel Peace Prize Acceptance Speech

Connecting with the Book

How does Wiesel's affirmation of his faith in God compare with his attitude toward God during his imprisonment in the death camps?

1. What qualities do you admire most about Elie Wiesel? Why?

2. What is the effect of Wiesel's reference to the "young Jewish boy" in the third person, rather than to himself in the first person?

3. What does Wiesel mean by the statement that "No one is as capable of gratitude as one who has emerged from the kingdom of night"?

4. What are some examples of injustice and suffering that cry out for the world's attention today?

READING CHECK

a. According to the introduction to the speech, how will Wiesel use the Nobel Prize money?

b. In Wiesel's opinion, at what point do "national borders and sensitivities become irrelevant"?

c. What does Wiesel say is the "most insidious danger of all"?

Name _____ Date _____

TEST PART I: OBJECTIVE QUESTIONS

In the space provided, mark each true statement _T_ and each false statement _F_.
(20 points)

_____ **1.** Moché the Beadle tells the villagers in Sighet not to worry about the Nazis.

_____ **2.** Eliezer is the only son in a family of four children.

_____ **3.** During the transport to Auschwitz, Madame Schächter begins to scream because she imagines seeing piles of corpses.

_____ **4.** Kapos are prisoners given command over fellow prisoners.

_____ **5.** Eliezer tells the guards at Birkenau that he is 16 years old.

_____ **6.** Eliezer is whipped because he steals soup from a pot in the middle of the camp.

_____ **7.** During the transport to Buchenwald, prisoners fight over bread.

_____ **8.** When Eliezer's father is sick with dysentery, he begs Eliezer for coffee.

_____ **9.** Eliezer's father might still have been alive when he was removed from his bed.

_____ **10.** Eliezer loses both parents and a sister in the camps.

Circle the letter of the answer that best completes the statement. _(10 points)_

11. Moché the Beadle instructs Eliezer in
    a. Jewish history   **c.** Hasidic songs
    b. the cabbala   **d.** Nazi propaganda

12. Prior to deportation, the Jews of Sighet
    a. are required to wear a yellow star of David   **c.** relocate into ghettos
    b. bury their valuable property   **d.** all of the above

13. When Eliezer is beaten by a factory foreman, he is comforted by
    a. a French girl   **c.** Juliek
    b. his father   **d.** the boy with "a face like an angel"

14. At Auschwitz, Eliezer observes Dr. Mengele
    a. operating on camp prisoners   **c.** selecting prisoners for the gas chamber
    b. shooting camp prisoners   **d.** pulling the gold crowns from prisoners' teeth

15. After their arrival at Buchenwald, Eliezer
    a. bribes another prisoner for a place   **c.** gets his father a place in the infirmary
    in his father's bunk
    b. gives his father a warm cup of coffee   **d.** prays for his father

Name _____ Date _____

 **PART II: SHORT-ANSWER QUESTIONS**

Answer each question, using the lines provided. (40 points)

16. Describe the experience of Moché the Beadle in the forest and the reaction of the villagers to his story when he returns to Sighet.

_____

_____

_____

17. What Biblical or historical allusions foreshadow the deportation of the Jews of Sighet?

_____

_____

_____

18. Explain the purpose of the "selection" and why Eliezer is advised to lie about his age when he enters Birkenau.

_____

_____

_____

19. Explain what causes the narrator to lose his faith in God his first night in the camps.

_____

_____

_____

20. Provide two examples of the narrator characterizing those he encounters by describing their eyes.

_____

_____

_____

TEST   PART II: SHORT-ANSWER QUESTIONS *(cont.)*

21. What is the reason for the march from Auschwitz to Buchenwald?

....

....

....

22. For what kind of strength does Eliezer pray after seeing Rabbi Eliahou in search of his son?

....

....

....

23. Describe the unusual event preceding the death of Juliek.

....

....

....

24. Briefly, what effect does the death of Eliezer's father have on Eliezer?

....

....

....

25. Describe in your own words what Eliezer sees in the mirror after his liberation.

....

....

....

TEST PART III: ESSAY QUESTIONS

Choose two of the following topics. Use your own paper to write two or three paragraphs about each topic you choose. *(30 points)*

a. Twice, the narrator interjects events that occurred after the war as commentary on events during the war. Choose one such event, describe it in detail, and explain its effect on the account as a whole.

b. Explain how *Night* addresses the subject of dignity in the face of inhuman cruelty. Support your answer with examples from the text. What theme do these examples develop?

c. The prisoners receive conflicting advice on how to survive in the camps: through self-interest or by helping each other. Explain each of these two strategies in relation to Eliezer's experience.

d. How does Eliezer's relationship to God change throughout the book?

e. Summarize what you have learned from *Night,* and tell what lessons, if any, you think the modern world has learned from it.

f. Discuss how one of the **Connections** from the back of the book (HRW LIBRARY edition) is related to a theme, issue, or character in *Night.*

Use this space to make notes.

Answer Key

Answer Key

Part I

■ Making Meanings

> **READING CHECK**
>
> **a.** He goes to the synagogue.
>
> **b.** Moché and Eliezer talk about God and prayer.
>
> **c.** Moché the Beadle is deported as a foreign Jew.
>
> **d.** The Jews of Sighet were living in ghettos.
>
> **e.** Madame Schächter sees fire.

1. Responses will vary. Possible responses include that the atrocities described are too inhuman to believe, or that the Jews of Sighet could not imagine or admit that they too could be victims of such treatment.

2. Allusion to the expulsion of the Jews from Judah by the Babylonians foreshadows the deportation of the Jewish community of Sighet, first from their homes and then from the ghettos, by the German army.

3. Responses will vary. Students may note that their relationship is not demonstrative, but seems respectful. His father is rather unemotional and not enthusiastic about Eliezer's interest in studying the cabbala. Eliezer recognizes without resentment his father's position in the community and the responsibility of being an only son.

4. Though Moché the Beadle survived the execution in the forest, something inside of him died. The man with "dreaming eyes" that Eliezer chose for a master returns to Sighet changed. The joy has gone from his eyes; he closes them or walks with his eyes downcast to avoid looking into the faces of those who will not believe his story.

5. Prior to the German occupation of Sighet, night is a time for Eliezer to study the cabbalistic books with Moché. However, once the German occupation dominates Eliezer's life, night becomes the backdrop for terror. News of deportation comes

at midnight. The transport to Auschwitz is described as "[a]n endless night." It is against the night sky that the prisoners first see the flames of Auschwitz.

6. It is ironic that although the act of wearing the star of David does not harm the wearer, the action was not harmless because the star symbolized Judaism and identified the wearer as a target of Nazi extermination.

7. Responses will vary. One example is Madame Schächter's screams about fire, which foreshadow the fires from the crematory at Auschwitz.

8. Responses will vary. Students may mention that the behavior of Madame Schächter's son is normal under the circumstances. The violent reactions of the prisoners on the transport to Birkenau are normal in the face of fears that are extreme and treatment beyond the boundaries of generally recognized human interaction.

9. Responses will vary, but most students will probably agree that Wiesel was so emotionally ruined by the experience that any attempt to write about it would have been a failure. The decade of waiting may have helped him gain some measure of perspective and enabled him to arrive at the unadorned style that makes the book so effective. Some students may feel that such horrors should have been revealed immediately, letting the world know as soon as possible about the atrocities.

■ Reading Strategies Worksheet

Understanding a Motif

(Responses will vary, but possible responses follow.)

A. Connotations for *night* include mysterious, scary, evil, romantic, haunted, imaginary, and dreamlike.

B.1. *Quotation:* "He was stooped from long nights of study."

Event: Eliezer awakens an old man and warns him about deportation.

Connotation: Night as a time for uncovering or studying mystery, a pursuit which may have been in vain.

2. *Quotation:* "Night. No one prayed, so that the night would pass quickly."

Event: Tension–filled waiting, the night before deportation.

Connotation: Night as a time of terrible suspense, a darkness to be endured, an unpleasant passage to dawn.

3. *Quotation:* "An endless night."

Event: Madame Schächter's screaming visions on the way to Birkenau.

Connotation: Night as the time of nightmares, visions of destruction from which it is impossible to wake.

FOLLOW-UP: Responses will vary. The shift in the manner in which the narrator looks at night, first as a time of prayer and illumination and then as a time of fear and confusion, reflects the change that is coming over his life and will forever alter it. The world he has always known dies, and with it a part of Eliezer dies as well.

Part II

■ Making Meanings

READING CHECK

a. Eliezer's single thought is to remain with his father.

b. Eliezer tells the guards he is an eighteen-year-old farmer.

c. Eliezer tells his mother's nephew that the nephew's family in Antwerp is safe.

d. Eliezer and his father work in an electronics warehouse.

e. A French girl shows kindness to Eliezer.

f. The two adults and the child are accused of stockpiling weapons.

1. Responses will vary. Students may mention the overwhelming presence of death, the dehumanizing conditions, the heartless treatment, or the general sense of doom.

2. After seeing the burning ditches full of bodies, the newly arrived prisoners realize that that too could be their fate. They recite the Kaddish for the dead and for themselves. In response to the horror of what they see, the prisoners turn immediately to their faith. Eliezer's struggle begins with his inability to rationalize praying to a God he believes allowed this scale of murder to occur.

3. The narrator characterizes people by describing their eyes: His father's eyes grow dim in camp; the officer who shows kindness to the children has a smile in his eyes; the French girl who shows Eliezer kindness is later recognized by her "dreamy eyes"; Franek, the foreman, who extorts a gold-crowned tooth from Eliezer, has eyes that "gleamed with desire."

4. Responses will vary. The small joys of greeting familiar faces, the kindness of "human words" by the block commander, Eliezer's effort to protect his relative from the truth about his family, and the young French girl at the factory help the prisoners maintain a sense of dignity despite the dehumanizing conditions of the camps.

5. Responses will vary. Students may note that in the course of his first night, Wiesel explains that the "instincts of self-preservation, of self-defense, of pride, had all deserted us." Yet later on, it is concern for himself that prevents him from helping his father while his father is being beaten. Students should also note the story of the *pipel* who forsook his commitment to his family and beat his own father for failure to make his bed properly.

6. Ironically, due to the physical duress experienced daily and the mental stress of "selection," the threat of death that the air raid signals does not worry the prisoners. Instead, they are happy that the Nazis are vulnerable to attack.

7. Responses will vary. The imagery of night is extended by the description of camp experiences as nightmares from which he would never awake and of the "nocturnal silence which deprived [him], for all eternity, of the desire to live."

8. The devout boy interested in becoming a rabbi is so profoundly affected by the death he witnesses at Auschwitz that his faith dies: "Never shall I forget those flames which consumed my faith forever." He considers himself afflicted like Job, though unlike Job, he turns away from prayer.

9. Old prisoners beg the younger ones not to lose faith. Some prisoners cling to Hasidic songs and numerology to survive. Some see the persecution as a test from God.

10. Responses will vary. Students might cite *The Diary of Anne Frank,* which conveys the themes of self-preservation and family commitment and the struggle of faith; the musical *Fiddler on the Roof,* which conveys the themes of family commitment and dignity in the face of cruelty; and Pablo Picasso's painting *Guernica,* which conveys the theme of dignity in the face of cruelty.

11. Responses will vary, but students may tend to agree that slogans offer easy answers for unthinking people. Slogans usually suggest simplistic courses of action that do not account for individual differences and circumstances, reducing complex situations and ideas to a few clever words. Rulers through the ages have realized the power of slogans to control the masses.

■ Reading Strategies Worksheet

Internal Conflict
Responses will vary, but possible responses follow.

First Oval: Hearing the recital of the Kaddish, Wiesel "revolts" against God "for the first time." He questions why he should bless God's name, why he should thank God.

Comment: It seems a natural response to question one's faith in the face of such incredible horror. It is surprising, however, that Wiesel blames God and not simply the evil in other human beings.

Second oval: Wiesel says that he sees God in the person of the young prisoner hanging on the gallows.
Comment: The vision of God on the gallows is an ironic echo of the Christian Crucifixion. Here, however, instead of Christ dying to redeem humanity, the prisoner represents to Eliezer the death of God.

FOLLOW-UP: Responses will vary. Some students may feel that writing allows one to explore his or her emotions, to study those emotions carefully, and to resolve the conflict. Others may think that writing can only help resolve internal conflict after time has provided sufficient distance and objectivity. If responses are personal, they need not be shared with the class.

Part III

■ Making Meanings

> **READING CHECK**
> a. Eliezer's father wants him to save his strength and Eliezer no longer wishes to participate in religious celebrations.
> b. Eliezer's foot is infected.
> c. The prisoners in the infirmary are liberated shortly after the other prisoners evacuate for Buchenwald.
> d. Juliek plays Beethoven on his violin just before he dies.
> e. Twelve prisoners complete the journey to Buchenwald.
> f. It is probable that Eliezer's father dies of dysentery and a blow to the head by the guard.
> g. The prisoners revolt and drive the SS from the camp shortly before U.S. troops arrive.

1. Responses will vary. Students may feel that Eliezer does all that he can for his father and should not blame himself or assume he could have done anything more. Some may find his inability to

grieve understandable and perhaps conducive to maintaining his own morale in order to survive. Students may feel that Eliezer lost his struggle with himself by not coming to his father's side when his father calls his name, and they may find it hard to understand why, after trying to stay with his father throughout the time in the camps, he now does not grieve at their separation.

2. Eliezer rejects God while others are celebrating Rosh Hashanah through a series of questions, which is how Moché the Beadle said that man raises himself to God. Perhaps Eliezer's struggle is, in a way, a celebration.

3. When Akiba Drumer loses his faith, his eyes become blank—emotionally, he dies. The loss of spiritual strength affects him physically; according to the narrator, he self-selects himself for extermination.

4. Responses will vary. The head of the block, despite all the indignities that he has witnessed and experienced, wants the liberating army to realize that the prisoners did not become animals in the face of dehumanizing treatment.

5. Responses will vary. Students may feel that Eliezer favors family commitment over self-preservation because he stays with his father, trying to meet his father's needs as best as he can. However, the loss of his father robs him of purpose. The narrator's presentation of the father and son on the transport to Buchenwald shows little sympathy toward those concerned only with self-preservation. Eliezer is more understanding of the self-preserving choice that the son of Rabbi Eliahou makes, but he prays that he will resist such an urge. Some students may feel that the author admits the power of self-preservation: Eliezer does acknowledge that he is more concerned about himself than about his father when his father is being beaten. Students may also feel that the circumstances place an unreasonable burden on family commitment.

6. The decline of Eliezer's father can be traced through his eyes. First they are "tired" and "veiled with despair," but while they are in the brick factory seeking shelter his eyes are described as "petrified." On the train, it is only the slight movement of his eyelids that indicates he is alive and saves him from being thrown from the train. The "light of thankfulness in his eyes" for Eliezer's kindness gives way to a "visionary gaze," and shortly thereafter he dies.

7. Responses will vary. Students may feel that the rush for bread and physical comfort is completely natural and understandable, overwhelming any desire for immediate vengeance. Students may believe that the absence of vengefulness is perhaps the clearest indicator of the emotional death that Wiesel describes. Some students may also feel that Wiesel oversimplifies the emotional state of the victims when he asserts that none of them gave any thought at all to either their families or to vengeance.

8. Responses will vary. The final image of Eliezer's mirrored face reflects an emotional death that his physical survival could not prevent.

9. Responses will vary, but students should be urged to avoid easy generalizations. The wartime events revealed an enormous range of human behavior, from cruelty to heroism, from selfishness to selflessness. Students may comment that the war and the Holocaust demonstrated that people are capable of almost any imaginable act under unusual circumstances, that "civilization" has not progressed as far as it sometimes seems to have, and that people still have to be protected from the basest motives of other people.

10. Responses will vary, with most students probably agreeing that the ending is effective because of its abruptness. The sudden ending suggests the wordless shock that Wiesel and the other prisoners experienced. With time, the survivors would

be able to express themselves. Some students might suggest that Wiesel should have told more about the details of the liberation, the responses of the Allied armies, and the end of the war.

■ Reading Strategies Worksheet

■ Theme

Yet on Rosh Hashanah, ten thousand prisoners, including the Kapos, gather to celebrate the New Year. Despite their hunger, they set aside their soup until after the services. The prisoners wish each other a Happy New Year, taking joy in the tradition.

Yet Juliek managed to play music before his death. Somehow he managed to survive the march with his violin and keep it intact. His final concert is a fierce expression of dignity, because he plays the music of Beethoven, a composer who celebrates human freedom and individuality, and whose music the Nazis have forbidden Jews to play.

Yet Eliezer sacrifices his bread ration to secure a bunk near his father and continues to give his father some of his rations despite the old man's imminent death. Eliezer resists the temptation to abandon his father.

FOLLOW-UP: Responses will vary. The actions do indicate stubborn resistance to dehumanization and attempts to maintain self-respect and human values. Though the prisoners have no control over many aspects of their life, to wait to eat their thick soup is an exercise of the control that they do have. Juliek clings to his music for the solace and beauty it can provide; his playing of Beethoven is a small act of rebellion. Though logic would dictate that Eliezer not waste his rations on his father, the power of family commitment is a higher human value. Statements of them may vary, but should focus on the idea that dignity offers a way to resist the dehumanizing effects of extreme cruelty.

Literary Elements Worksheets

■ Motif

1. Moché the Beadle; dreamy and then joyless; he is a kind and understanding teacher before he is deported, but he returns to Sighet an emotionally dead man.

2. Madame Schächter; burning eyes; her behavior is crazed, and she screams about fires.

3. The French girl; dreamy eyes; she is kind to Eliezer.

4. Franek and the old man on the transport to Buchenwald; gleaming eyes; both men are greedy. Franek extorts Eliezer's gold-crowned tooth, and the old man snatches bread.

5. Eliezer; eyes of a corpse; he declares himself dead.

FOLLOW-UP

- Another character with dreamy eyes is the old scholar that Eliezer awakens in the middle of the night to warn about deportation. It appears that those with dreamy eyes are kind; Moché and the old man are both students of the Jewish holy books, as Eliezer had aspired to be.

■ Theme

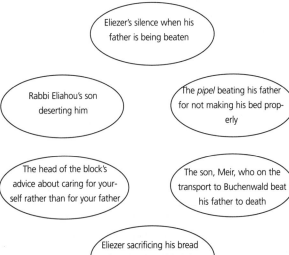

Eliezer's silence when his father is being beaten

Rabbi Eliahou's son deserting him

The *pipel* beating his father for not making his bed properly

The head of the block's advice about caring for yourself rather than for your father

The son, Meir, who on the transport to Buchenwald beat his father to death

Eliezer sacrificing his bread ration in order to be in the bunk near his father

FOLLOW-UP: Responses will vary. The narrator admits his own selfishness and the fear that caused his behavior, a fear that kept him alive. He remains remarkably nonjudgmental about other children and their parents, but most students may find him on the side of family commitment. The *pipel* and Meir have grown crazed, and it is easy to find their behavior undesirable. Students should recognize that it is the *balance* of the concern for self and the concern for others that helps Eliezer survive. The devotion to his father gave him the strength not to succumb to the release of physical death. *Night*'s theme on this topic is that only by maintaining family commitment can one's soul survive great hardships.

■ Tone

Possible responses: witnessing the beating of Madame Schächter by the other prisoners; never seeing his mother again; having a number engraved on his arm; hearing Juliek play Beethoven; waking to find his father had been taken away during the night. **FOLLOW-UP:** Responses will vary, but many students may feel the need to provide their own comments on the events. This is the effect that Wiesel probably intends, presenting facts so shocking that the reader is compelled to respond emotionally and venture into the interpretations that Wiesel could not bear to make.

Vocabulary Worksheets

■ Vocabulary Worksheet 1

Parts I and II: Sighet to Buna

If you wish to score these worksheets, assign the point values given in parentheses.

A. *(5 points each)*

1. d. explaining in detail	**6.** b. savage
2. b. clarity	**7.** d. nighttime
3. a. required	**8.** a. constantly
4. a. ignoble	**9.** c. shriveled
5. c. theoretical concept	**10.** c. official order

B. 11–15 *(5 points each)* Responses will vary.

C. *(5 points each)*

16. a. authors : write

17. c. investigation : examination

18. c. charity : kindness

19. b. revered : admiration

20. a. musical : inharmonious

■ Vocabulary Worksheet 2

Part III: Buna to Buchenwald

A. *(5 points each)*

1. b. endless	**6.** d. burden
2. a. extremely thin	**7.** c. unimportant
3. b. scorn	**8.** b. watchfulness
4. c. promptly	**9.** a. subtle
5. a. amazed	**10.** d. motionless

B. 11–20 *(5 points each)* Responses will vary.

Exploring the Connections

■ The Mourner's Kaddish

> **READING CHECK**
> The prayer asks for life.

1. The prayer places God's will above human concerns, and it asks for peace to replace the pain of loss.

2. Responses may vary. The repetition of words, the short and stately lines, and the intense expression of feeling lend a lyric quality to the prayer.

Connecting with the Book

Responses will vary. Students may say that Eliezer might have resented the entire prayer for its glorification of a God that he felt had abandoned him and others in the death camp.

■ A Spring Morning

> **READING CHECK**
>
> **a.** The trucks have come to transport the Jews to their deaths.
>
> **b.** He hopes to leave her behind unnoticed and thereby save her life.
>
> **c.** She is shot and killed.

1. Responses will vary. Students may say they admire the courage and dignity with which the family accepts their fate; others may say they admire the parents' concern for their daughter.

2. Students may list images such as the sun breaking through the clouds; the child sleeping peacefully, "round and large and rosy as an apple"; the town "washed clean" by the rain; the peaceful Sunday morning; the girl's soft cheeks; the green trees. The images of beauty, innocence, and peace are opposed to the horror, guilt, and terror of the situation.

3. They add to the tension by suspending the present time and giving the reader glimpses into happier, more innocent, times in Aron's life. They make the present all the more mournful.

4. The detailed description of the circumstances around the death of the girl slow down the final scene: the man felt his wife's fingers, and heard her moan; he turned slowly; he saw the smoke from the gunshot wafting on the air; his steps seemed interminable; he stroked his daughter's hair before lifting her body to carry on the march.

5. The tone of the short story is more emotional and more overtly dramatic than Wiesel's *Night*.

Connecting with the Book

Wiesel uses the image of "night" to symbolize the physical and spiritual darkness that befell him and other prisoners during the Holocaust. This story echoes that symbolism in the statement "Night was slipping away,

though what was this new day but night, the blackest of black nights, cruel, and filled with torment."

■ The Berlin-Bucharest Express

> **READING CHECK**
>
> **a.** Bronia delivered falsified papers and passports to Polish Jews so that they could escape capture by the Nazis.
>
> **b.** The secretary was afraid that because of her dark complexion, she would be mistaken for a Jew and imprisoned by the Nazis.
>
> **c.** The officer had issued a command to kill innocent Jewish men, women, and children.

1. Students may say that they feel more sympathy for Bronia, because she cannot convince the town leaders of the Nazi danger and because she carries the memories of the killings in Zhitomir. Some may pity the officer who feels he is forced to follow inhumane orders.

2. The mention of the precise time that the train stopped in the town, the images of December snow falling, the crowded train, the dim light in the train, and the "cold, sorrowful December night" contribute to the realism, the tension, and the sadness of the story.

3. Responses will vary. Students may mention questions such as these: Why didn't the officer refuse to order his men to kill innocent people? What would he do with the documents and pictures? What would become of the officer?

4. Perhaps the officer fears that he will be shot if the picture is traced to him.

5. Responses will vary. Students may say that the officer might have been shot for not following orders. Nevertheless, he might have tried to organize other officers to resist the killing. They may speculate that his fear for his own safety overrode his concern for the innocent people of Zhitomir.

Connecting with the Book

The town leaders of Slotwina Brzesko repeatedly tell Bronia that such horrors could not happen in their town because Nazis were killing only Jews in formerly held Russian territories. In spite of Bronia's report, they refuse to believe that their Jewish community could be in danger. Similarly, the people of Sighet "refused not only to believe [Moché's] stories, but even to listen to them." They claimed that Moché was making up the stories to gain sympathy.

■ Maus

READING CHECK

a. Being near the end of the line increased one's chance of getting solid food, which had sunk to the bottom of the soup.

b. The prisoner claimed to be German.

1. Responses will vary. Students may note that the subject of the excerpt is serious and the author/illustrator does not attempt to add levity to the account. The expressions on the faces of the mice and the guard convey the appropriate human emotions: disappointment, fear, and rage.

2. Animal characters make it easier to distance oneself from the tragedy in order to better understand and learn about the experience of the prisoners. It is appropriate too that the inhuman cruelty and dehumanization that occurred at the concentration camps be portrayed by non-humans.

3. The narrative style of *Maus* is that of an interview. The son of a survivor is interviewing his father about the experience. The first, sixth, and eleventh frames show the two in discussion.

4. Responses will vary. Students may find that the way in which the story is told in broken English lends authenticity to the account and creates a mood of "hearing" the interview take place. The fact that the author does not correct his father's

broken English lends credibility to the account by making it easier for readers to accept the accuracy of other details in the account.

5. By the placement of the hands and the expression on the faces it appears that Spiegelman is presenting the prisoner as a Jew and not the German he claims to be. From the text and by the illustrations it is clear, however, that whether he is Jewish or German is irrelevant to the guard who kills him.

Connecting with the Book

The mood of *Maus* is matched by the mood in *Night*. The dark drawings, the subject matter, and the father/son theme are reflected in *Night*.

■ The Treblinka Revolt

READING CHECK

a. The barracks are named for a German officer killed by a young Jewish man.

b. They decided to start the revolt early because the participants were agitated and unable to "keep the secret."

1. Responses will vary. Students who were not aware that prisoners in concentration camps had rebelled against their captors may find the memoir surprising. Other students may have already been aware of such revolts, or may have assumed that some prisoners must have taken such actions.

2. The story of the Jewish youth who killed SS man Max Brill to avenge the deaths of his wife and child foreshadows the revolt's attempt to avenge the deaths of many thousands of Jews at Treblinka. Kohn even identifies the unnamed youth as "our ideal."

3. By describing the atrocities of Treblinka from the point of view of the rebels, Kohn makes the reader aware of the mounting anger of the prisoners and helps the reader understand, as far as possible, the desire for revenge.

4. Franz's statement tells the reader that the Nazis intended to murder every single Jew, not only in Europe but in the entire world. The speech is "significant" because it reinforces the prisoners' belief that they have no option other than to revolt against their captors, despite the overwhelming odds against their success.

5. The details of the plans for the revolt build a degree of suspense, because they are so complicated and because so many things could go wrong.

6. The author takes satisfaction in the large number of German casualties. The rebels also destroyed the killing facilities and the Max Brill barracks.

Connecting with the Book

Comparisons with Wiesel's description of Auschwitz and Buna:

- Both mention imprisoned Jews in service to the Nazis.
- Both mention prisoners having to strip before entering the gas chambers.

Contrasts to Wiesel's description of Buna:

- The attitude of active revenge among prisoners is more fierce at Treblinka.
- Prisoners had greater latitude to move about German facilities at Treblinka.
- There is a fake rail station at Treblinka; such a decoy is not described by Wiesel.
- The Treblinka prisoners were able to execute at least a somewhat successful rebellion.

■ Mauthausen May 1945/My Black Messiah

> **READING CHECK**
>
> **a.** The writer and Edzia were sick with typhus.
>
> **b.** The Kapos, guards, and SS disappeared from the camp.
>
> **c.** The soldier saw the horrors of what the Nazis had done to people in the death camps.

1. Responses will vary. Some students may say the image of the girls struggling up the hill to the death camp was most powerful; others may mention the description of the face of the African American soldier.

2. Responses will vary. Students may say that phrases such as "stared with eyes that didn't see,"* "froze in place,"* and "flood of devastating pain"* help the reader picture the shock of the soldier.

3. Responses will vary. Students may say she means that it takes strength to live, hope, and smile after experiencing and seeing the atrocities of the Holocaust.

4. In Jewish tradition the Messiah is the promised deliverer or savior, who will rescue the Jewish people and usher in an era of peace and prosperity. For the speaker of the poem, the African American soldier delivered her from the hands of the Nazis and certain death.

Connecting with the Book

According to Weitz, the guards at Mauthausen disappeared, and American soldiers liberated the camp the next day. She emphasizes the shocked expressions on the faces of the Americans. Wiesel describes days of chaos preceding the liberation. He also tells of the takeover of the camp by the resistance and the flight of the Germans, after which the camp was liberated by the Americans. Like Weitz, Wiesel was ill near the time of the liberation.

*From "My Black Messiah" from "Mauthausen, May 1945" from *I Promised I Would Tell* by Sonia Schreiber Weitz, edited by Susan Belt Cogley. Copyright © 1993 by Sonia Schreiber Weitz. Reprinted by permission of ***Facing History and Ourselves.***

Answer Key (cont.)

■The Yellow Star

READING CHECK

a. The Buchenwald prisoners wanted to track down the SS guards and bring them to justice.

b. The *Mussulmänner* were former prisoners too injured or ill to survive.

c. The narrator gave tours of the camp to soldiers and helped bury the dead.

d. The spectacle of thousands of liberated Jews reaffirming their faith at Shavuot services inspired the narrator's faith.

1. Responses will vary. Students may mention his resurgence of faith—an experience different from that of Wiesel in *Night.*

2. Students may mention the reactions of the SS guards upon being captured by the former prisoners; the fact that some prisoners were too ill to appreciate their liberation; the death of some prisoners from eating too much; or Unsdorfer's religious revival amid the horrors of Buchenwald.

3. Wiesel gives few details of the days after the liberation, whereas Unsdorfer cites many details. Unlike Unsdorfer, Wiesel recalls no one acting out of revenge. Like Wiesel, Unsdorfer tells of people getting sick from eating too much or from eating tainted food.

4. Responses will vary. Students may say that in spite of tremendous suffering and deprivation, people can remain strong in their religious faith.

Connecting with the Book

After witnessing the atrocious deaths of so many innocents, Wiesel could not give glory to God; hearing others recite the words of the Kaddish or seeing them celebrate Rosh Hashanah confirmed this realization. For Unsdorfer, the Kaddish raised questions of the survival of the Jewish people. Could the "Jewish nation, . . . religion and heritage" continue to thrive after the Nazi assault? The celebration of Shavuot reestablished for the author his faith and his confidence in its survival.

■ The Trial of the Century

READING CHECK

a. The United States, Britain, France, and the Soviet Union brought charges against Nazi leaders.

b. Their case had to bridge dissimilar legal systems, languages, and political objectives. Also, the defendants were charged with crimes that were not specified in any of the Allied countries' laws.

c. Jackson won convictions against all but three of the defendants.

1. Responses will vary. Some students may say that they would have wanted to watch such an important trial. Others may say that hearing testimony about Nazi atrocities would have been too difficult to witness.

2. Responses will vary. Students may say that the writer uses any two of these: facts and statistics (facts about the defendants, the indictments, and the chief prosecutor, for example); quotations such as those by chief prosecutor Jackson, assistant prosecutor, and Holocaust survivor Sprecher; specific examples such as descriptions of dramatic moments during the trial and a description of ways that Jackson "lost his edge"; and anecdotes (Stalin's suggestion and the discovery of the buried notebooks).

3. Students may say that the defendants based their claim on the fact that they were not present when crimes were committed, or that they were merely following orders.

4. Responses will vary. Some students may say that the trials had little influence, because of the atrocities that have since taken place in Cambodia, Rwanda, Argentina, Bosnia, and other countries. Others may note that the trials provided a way to identify crimes against humanity.

Connecting with the Book

Responses will vary. Some students may mention the hanging of the young boy with the face of a "sad-eyed angel" at Buna. Others may say that Wiesel might have told of the process of selection in the death camps or the march in the snow to Buchenwald.

■ But in the night

> **READING CHECK**
>
> **a.** The speaker's dreams allow her to be with loved ones who have died.
>
> **b.** The poet speaks of her sister, brother, and husband.

1. Responses will vary. Some students may mention the images of "little children wailing," of a head lying protectively on someone's heart, of the dawn "strewn with the red seed of the sun," or of night that has "cried itself out into the day."

2. Responses will vary. Students may note that there is a tone of longing, anxiety, grief, and humility. The tone may also be described as compassionate, profoundly sad, or nightmarish.

3. Responses will vary. A possible response: In daylight I can stop thinking about those I have lost.

4. As night, the time in which the speaker can feel the presence of her loved ones, draws to a close, she wakes from her dreams and her loved ones seem to die all over again.

Connecting with the Book

Responses will vary. Some students may feel that Wiesel was afraid of misrepresenting prisoners' experiences and therefore remained silent. He may not have wished to carry the burden or may not have felt worthy of being a voice for millions who did not survive.

■ Babii Yar

> **READING CHECK**
>
> **a.** The speaker identifies with Anne Frank.
>
> **b.** The speaker says that they look threatening and seem like judges.

1. Responses will vary. Students may note that they find Yevtushenko's poem effective because, even though the poet is not Jewish, he seems particularly sensitive to Jewish suffering throughout the ages.

2. Responses will vary. Students may say that using the first-person point of view makes the incidents described in the poem seem more powerful and immediate.

3. Yevtushenko traces the history of Jewish persecution to emphasize that to build a sports stadium on this site would be an insult and would once again deny the suffering of the Jewish people.

4. Responses will vary. Students may infer that anti-Jewish attitudes prevailed in the former Soviet Union even after the Holocaust.

Connecting with the Book

Responses may vary. Students may assert that it is impossible to identify with Eliezer but certainly possible to feel compassion for him because of shared universal emotions: love, respect, fear, courage, and desire for self-preservation.

■ An Inner Freedom

> **READING CHECK**
>
> **a.** Frankl believes that humans have the ability to choose their attitude in any set of circumstances; they can overcome apathy and preserve spiritual freedom and independence of mind, or they can succumb to their circumstances.
>
> **b.** The speaker heard the tree say, "I am here—I am here—I am life, eternal life."

1. Responses will vary. Students may agree with Frankl that, at the very least, one may choose one's *attitude*. Others may feel that circumstances can overwhelm even strong spirits.

2. Responses will vary. Students may say that the direct and personal evidence lends more credibility to the conclusions.

3. Responses and examples will vary. Students may think that this account addresses the indomitable human spirit in the references to prisoners comforting one another, sharing their food, and facing imprisonment and death with courage.

4. Responses may vary, but students should understand that people who retain the ability to decide how they will act, despite great hardships, are "worthy of [their] suffering."

Connecting with the Book

Responses will vary. Students may mention examples such as that of Rabbi Eliahou, whose face "shone with his inner purity," or Juliek, who played his violin before he died.

■ A Cambodian Nightmare

> **READING CHECK**
>
> **a.** The Khmer Rouge wanted to turn Cambodia into an agrarian commune.
>
> **b.** They wanted to destroy educated and thinking people: intellectuals, professionals, and religious and civic leaders.
>
> **c.** Cambodian cultural beliefs include a dedication to community; an emphasis on devotion, discipline, and gratitude; patience with hardship; trust in neighbors; and a belief in fate.

1. Responses will vary. Students may mention some of these: shock, outrage, disbelief, sadness, sorrow, admiration, and respect.

2. Many of the Cambodians who might have told the story were killed; also, according to the article, Cambodians tend not to discuss painful memories, and they lack the anger which often motivates Holocaust victims to recount their story.

3. Students may speculate that the Thai government felt that it could not support so many immigrants. Prejudice may also have been a factor.

4. Responses will vary. Talking or writing about an experience allows the survivor to process feelings or to reconnect with the community by promoting understanding. Some reasons for remaining silent are that words often seem inadequate to describe the experience, that the survivors would rather not relive their experience by retelling the events, or that words can be considered a disservice to the dead.

Connecting with the Book

The Cambodians have little anger toward the Khmer Rouge, believing that it is their karma, or fate, to have suffered. Many of the Jews described in *Night* feel repressed rage and anger toward the Nazis. Wiesel, however, makes a point of the absence of vengeance immediately after liberation.

■ Why *Do* They Visit?

> **READING CHECK**
>
> **a.** The museum opened in April 1993.
>
> **b.** They thought that only survivors and their families, Jewish students, and temple groups would come. They also questioned the relevance of a museum based on "European savagery" amid monuments to American democracy.
>
> **c.** Visitors see a large picture of American soldiers staring at a pile of corpses in a concentration camp.

1. Responses will vary. Students may want to visit in order to honor the memory of the dead; others may fear the horror of the history.

2. The author is informing readers about the museum and about reasons for visiting the museum.

He provides background information and describes images of museum displays. He also provides quotations from critics and supporters of the museum and poses questions that are provoked by museum displays.

3. According to the article, contemporary U.S. citizens are drawn to the study of the Holocaust because it represents an absolute in "an age of relativity"—an absolute evil which implies the possibility of absolute good.

4. Responses will vary. Students may say that all humans have the potential for good and evil and that the Holocaust is part of a "continuum" of violence. They may also quote the writer: ". . . man is not irredeemably evil . . . acts of free will and courage are possible."

Connecting with the Book

Studying *Night* in school involves students in looking at the Holocaust experience at both the emotional and analytical levels. Wiesel's account, the narratives presented at the museum, pictures from the era, and rebuilt barracks and gas chambers vividly bring the human aspect of suffering to the reader and the visitor. Some students might remark that visual presentations have an impact that is unavoidable and for some people, more powerful than reading a book.

■ Nobel Peace Prize Acceptance Speech

READING CHECK

a. Wiesel will use the money to set up a foundation that pays for conferences on human rights.

b. They become irrelevant when human lives are endangered and human dignity is in jeopardy.

c. According to Wiesel, indifference is the most insidious danger.

---

1. Responses will vary. Students may say that they admire his selfless dedication to human rights. Others may say they admire his ability to articu-

late his devastating experience and make people aware of the dangers of indifference.

2. In speaking of himself in the third person, Wiesel makes his own lost youth a symbol of universal loss; at the same time, he refers to the future of his own fourteen-year-old son standing beside him during the speech.

3. Wiesel means that those who have seen the worst in human behavior and have been deprived of everything—families and friends, adequate food and clothing, dignity and faith—are more able to appreciate large and small graces and kindnesses.

4. Responses will vary. Students may mention both international conflicts and examples of prejudice in the United States.

Connecting with the Book

As he watched babies being murdered in the fires at Birkenau and the hangings at Buna, Wiesel felt that his faith in God had been murdered. Years later, his faith in God has been restored to the point that Wiesel feels that "without it no action would be possible."

Test

■ Part I

1. F	**6.** F	**11.** b
2. T	**7.** T	**12.** d
3. F	**8.** T	**13.** a
4. T	**9.** T	**14.** c
5. F	**10.** T	**15.** a

■ Part II

16. Moché witnesses a massacre by the Gestapo; he is shot in the leg and taken for dead. The Jews of Sighet dismiss his stories about the massacre and his warnings about the Germans.

17. Responses will vary. Students should mention one or more of the following: The expulsion of the Jews from Judah in the sixth century B.C. by the

Babylonians, foreshadowing their expulsion by the German army; the destruction of the Temple during the Babylonian captivity foreshadows the destruction of the Jews of Sighet's life, property, and synagogue during the German occupation; the Spanish Inquisition was a period of persecution or forced conversion of Jews and those considered heretical Christians during the 1400s, and in the same way the Jews are being singled out and tortured for their religious beliefs.

18. The selection determines which prisoners will go to the gas chambers. Eliezer is advised to lie about his age so that he will be sent to the labor camp instead of being killed immediately.

19. The sight of bodies of children and adults in a burning ditch causes Wiesel to lose his faith.

20. Responses may vary. Possible responses include: Moché, who is wise and becomes Eliezer's master in the mystical books, is first characterized by "dreaming eyes," but after returning to Sighet he has no joy in his eyes. Madame Schächter with "burning eyes" goes insane on the transport and screams about seeing fire. A head of the block who shows kindness to children has a smile in his eyes. Two characters who are greedy—a Kapo and an old man on the transport to Buchenwald—have a gleam in their eyes.

21. The Germans move the prisoners to Buchenwald to evade the advancing Russian army.

22. Eliezer prays that he will have the strength not to abandon his father as the rabbi's son has done.

23. Packed into the barracks at Gleiwitz, Eliezer hears Juliek playing Beethoven on his violin before he dies.

24. After his father dies, nothing matters to Eliezer; he loses his sense of purpose.

25. Responses may vary but students should suggest that Eliezer sees a "corpse" when he looks at his face in the mirror, a man spiritually and emotionally dead.

■ Part III

a. Responses will vary. Students should mention one of the following events:

- The account of meeting the French girl from the Buna warehouse (a Jew who passed as an Aryan) on the Paris Metro after the war interjects a moment of relief into the concentration camp narrative. The reader is reminded that Eliezer and others survived this ordeal and later experienced the somber joy of meeting other survivors. Her compassion was victorious over indifference.

- The scene of a tourist in Aden throwing money to native children and causing a deadly struggle is compared to German workmen throwing bread into the transport cars. This digression in the narration illustrates how the experiences of the war shape the narrator's assessment of human behavior after the war. He has come to realize that thoughtlessly cruel actions are not confined to wartime, and that people must be made aware of the consequences of their actions or inaction.

b. Instances of maintaining dignity in the face of inhuman cruelty include the continued practice of religious observances, the kindness of prisoners toward one another (advice to lie about age, the French girl, Eliezer protecting Rabbi Eliahou's feelings, humane Kapos), Juliek playing Beethoven, the head of the block cleaning the barracks before evacuation, and Eliezer's ceaseless sacrifices for his father. These examples demonstrate that, even under the most horrific circumstances, some small measure of human dignity is at least *possible.* They develop the theme that taking advantage of the tiniest opportunities to act like civilized and compassionate human beings is an enormous victory for the human spirit.

c. Responses will vary. Students may feel that the author's insight into the conflict between self-preservation and family commitment favors family commitment because he stays with his father, trying to meet his father's needs as best as he can, and because the loss of his father robs him of purpose. The narrator's presentation of the father and son on the transport to Buchenwald shows little sympathy toward those concerned only with self-preservation. Eliezer is more understanding of the self-preserving choice that the son of Rabbi Eliahou makes, but he still prays he will resist such an urge. Some students may feel that the author admits the power of self-preservation: Eliezer does acknowledge that he was more concerned about himself than about his father after the air raid in Buchenwald and when his father is being beaten. It is likely that *both* strategies enable Eliezer to survive.

d. Students should note that, at first, Eliezer is interested in studying the cabbala. He is enthralled with his faith and with God. This changes utterly when he arrives in Birkenau and sees the bodies of children burning in a ditch. He declares that his faith is consumed by those fires. He does not deny the existence of God, but he cannot comprehend God's love for humans. He finds a small measure of satisfaction in accusing God of injustices. Some students may conclude that Eliezer

declares God dead when he says that the young *pipel* being hanged on the scaffold is God; however, Eliezer later prays to God for the strength not to abandon his father. By the end of the book he is spiritually dead, but students may note that he regains his faith in subsequent years.

e. Responses will vary, but students might make the following observations: that human beings are capable of great good and great evil, that indifference to evil is itself evil, that prejudice must be carefully monitored and ultimately wiped out, that the testimonies of witnesses to cataclysmic events can serve to make people pay attention, that the future must be shaped with justice and compassion. Students may feel that the events of the Holocaust, as related by Wiesel and other survivors, have had an impact on the world's conscience and make it less likely that such an event could recur. Other students may feel that subsequent history shows that cruel people will continue to try to destroy innocent people if they can get away with it.

f. Responses will vary according to class interaction with the **Connections.**

The primary mission of the United States Holocaust Memorial Museum is to promote education about the history of the Holocaust and its implications for our lives today. This pamphlet is intended to assist educators who are preparing to teach Holocaust studies and related subjects.

Why Teach Holocaust History?

The history of the Holocaust represents one of the most effective, and most extensively documented, subjects for a pedagogical examination of basic moral issues. A structured inquiry into Holocaust history yields critical lessons for an investigation of human behavior. A study of the Holocaust also addresses one of the central tenets of education in the United States which is to examine what it means to be a responsible citizen. Through a study of the Holocaust, students can come to realize that:

- democratic institutions and values are not automatically sustained, but need to be appreciated, nurtured, and protected;
- silence and indifference to the suffering of others, or to the infringement of civil rights in any society, can—however, unintentionally—serve to perpetuate the problems; and
- the Holocaust was not an accident in history—it occurred because individuals, organizations, and governments made choices which not only legalized discrimination, but which allowed prejudice, hatred, and ultimately, mass murder to occur.

Questions of Rationale

Because the objective of teaching any subject is to engage the intellectual curiosity of the student in order to inspire critical thought and personal growth, it is helpful to structure your lesson plan on the Holocaust by considering throughout, questions of rationale. Before addressing what and how to teach, we would recommend that you contemplate the following:

- Why should students learn this history?

- What are the most significant lessons students can learn about the Holocaust?
- Why is a particular reading, image, document, or film an appropriate medium for conveying the lessons about the Holocaust which you wish to teach?

Among the various rationales offered by educators who have incorporated a study of the Holocaust into their various courses and disciplines are these:

- The Holocaust was a watershed event, not only in the 20th century, but in the entire history of humanity.
- Study of the Holocaust assists students in developing understanding of the ramifications of prejudice, racism, and stereotyping in any society. It helps students develop an awareness of the value of pluralism, and encourages tolerance of diversity in a pluralistic society.
- The Holocaust provides a context for exploring the dangers of remaining silent, apathetic, and indifferent in the face of others' oppression.
- Holocaust history demonstrates how a modern nation can utilize its technological expertise and bureaucratic infrastructure to implement destructive policies ranging from social engineering to genocide.
- A study of the Holocaust helps students think about the use and abuse of power, and the role and responsibilities of individuals, organizations, and nations when confronted with civil rights violations and/or policies of genocide.
- As students gain insight into the many historical, social, religious, political, and economic factors which cumulatively resulted in the Holocaust, they gain a perspective on how history happens, and how a convergence of factors can contribute to the disintegration of civilized values. Part of one's responsibility as a citizen in a democracy is to learn to identify the danger signals, and to know when to react.

When you, as an educator, take the time to consider the rationale for your lesson on the Holocaust, you will be more likely to select content that speaks to your students' interests and which provides them with a clearer understanding of the history. Most students demonstrate a high level of interest in studying the Holocaust precisely because the subject raises questions of fairness, justice, individual identity, peer pressure, conformity, indifference, and obedience—issues which adolescents confront in their daily lives. Students are also struck by the magnitude of the Holocaust, and the fact that so many people acting as collaborators, perpetrators, and bystanders allowed this genocide to occur by failing to protest or resist.

Methodological Considerations

1. Define what you mean by "Holocaust."

The Holocaust refers to a specific event in 20th century history: The systematic, bureaucratic annihilation of six million Jews by the Nazi regime and their collaborators as a central act of state during World War II. In 1933 approximately nine million Jews lived in the 21 countries of Europe that would be occupied by Germany during the war. By 1945 two out of every three European Jews had been killed. Although Jews were the primary victims, up to one half million Gypsies and at least 250,000 mentally or physically disabled persons were also victims of genocide. As Nazi tyranny spread across Europe from 1933 to 1945, millions of other innocent people were persecuted and murdered. More than three million Soviet prisoners of war were killed because of their nationality. Poles, as well as other Slavs, were targeted for slave labor, and as a result of the Nazi terror, almost two million perished. Homosexuals and others deemed "anti-social" were also persecuted and often murdered. In addition, thousands of political and religious dissidents such as communists, socialists, trade unionists, and Jehovah's Witnesses were persecuted for their beliefs and behavior and many of these individuals died as a result of maltreatment.

2. Avoid comparisons of pain.

A study of the Holocaust should always highlight the different policies carried out by the Nazi regime towards various groups of people; however, these distinctions should not be presented as a basis for comparison of suffering between them. Avoid generalizations which suggest exclusivity, such as "the victims of the Holocaust suffered the most cruelty ever faced by a people in the history of humanity." One cannot presume that the horror of an individual, family or community destroyed by the Nazis was any greater than that experienced by victims of other genocides.

3. Avoid simple answers to complex history.

A study of the Holocaust raises difficult questions about human behavior, and it often involves complicated answers as to why events occurred. Be wary of oversimplifications. Allow students to contemplate the various factors which contributed to the Holocaust; do not attempt to reduce Holocaust history to one or two catalysts in isolation from the other factors which came into play. For example, the Holocaust was not simply the logical and inevitable consequence of unbridled racism. Rather, racism, combined with centuries-old bigotry, renewed by a nationalistic fervor which emerged in Europe in the latter half of the 19th century, fueled by Germany's defeat in World War I and its national humiliation following the Treaty of Versailles, exacerbated by worldwide economic hard times, the ineffectiveness of the Weimar Republic, and international indifference, and catalyzed by the political charisma, militaristic inclusiveness, and manipulative propaganda of Adolf Hitler's Nazi regime, contributed to the eventuality of the Holocaust.

4. Just because it happened, doesn't mean it was inevitable.

Too often, students have the simplistic impression that the Holocaust was inevitable. Just because an historical event took place, and it was documented in textbooks and on film, does not mean that it had to happen. This seemingly obvious concept is often overlooked by students and teachers alike. The Holocaust took place because individuals, groups, and nations made decisions to act or not to act. By focusing on those decisions, we gain insight into history and human nature, and we can better help our students to become critical thinkers.

5. Strive for precision of language.

Any study of the Holocaust touches upon nuances of human behavior. Because of the complexity of the history, there is a temptation to overgeneralize and thus to distort the facts (e.g., "all concentration camps were killing centers" or "all Germans were collaborators"). Rather, teachers must strive to help students distinguish between categories of behavior and relevant historical references; to clarify the differences between prejudice and discrimination, collaborators and bystanders, armed and spiritual resistance, direct orders and assumed orders, concentration camps and killing centers, and guilt and responsibility.

Words that describe human behavior often have multiple meanings. Resistance, for example, usually refers to a physical act of armed revolt. During the Holocaust, it also meant partisan activism that ranged from smuggling messages, food, and weapons to actual military engagement. But, resistance also embraced willful disobedience: continuing to practice religious and cultural traditions in defiance of the rules; creating fine art, music and poetry inside ghettos and concentration camps. For many, simply maintain-

ing the will to remain alive in the face of abject brutality was the surest act of spiritual resistance.

6. Make careful distinctions about sources of information.

Students need practice in distinguishing between fact, opinion, and fiction; between primary and secondary sources, and between types of evidence such as court testimonies, oral histories, and other written documents. Hermeneutics—the science of interpretation—should be called into play to help guide your students in their analysis of sources. Students should be encouraged to consider why a particular text was written, who the intended audience was, whether there were any biases inherent in the information, any gaps in discussion, whether gaps in certain passages were inadvertent or not, and how the information has been used to interpret various events.

Because scholars often base their research on different bodies of information, varying interpretations of history can emerge. Consequently, all interpretations are subject to analytical evaluation. Only by refining their own "hermeneutic of suspicion" can students mature into readers who discern the difference between legitimate scholars who present competing historical interpretations, and those who distort or deny historical fact for personal or political gain.

7. Try to avoid stereotypical descriptions.

Though all Jews were targeted for destruction by the Nazis, the experiences of all Jews were not the same. Simplistic views and stereotyping take place when groups of people are viewed as monolithic in attitudes and actions. How ethnic groups or social clusters are labeled and portrayed in school curricula has a direct impact on how students perceive groups in their daily lives. Remind your students that although members of a group may share common experiences and beliefs, generalizations about them, without benefit of modifying or quali-fying terms (e.g., "sometimes," "usually," "in many cases but not all") tend to stereotype group behavior and distort historical reality. Thus, all Germans cannot be characterized as Nazis, nor should any nationality be reduced to a singular or one-dimensional description.

8. Do not romanticize history to engage students' interest.

One of the great risks of Holocaust education is the danger of fostering cynicism in our students by exposing them to the worst of human nature. Regardless, accuracy of fact must be a teacher's priority. People who risked their lives to rescue victims of Nazi oppression provide useful and important role models for students, yet an overemphasis on heroic tales in a unit on the Holocaust results in an inaccurate and unbal-anced account of the history. It is important to bear in mind that "at best, less than one-half of one percent of the total population [of non-Jews] under Nazi occupation helped to rescue Jews." [Oliner and Oliner, 1991, p. 363]

9. Contextualize the history you are teaching.

Events of the Holocaust, and particularly how indi-viduals and organizations behaved at that time, must be placed in an historical context so that stu-dents can begin to comprehend the circumstances that encouraged or discouraged these acts. Frame your approach to specific events and acts of com-plicity or defiance by considering when and where an act took place; the immediate consequences to oneself and one's family of assisting victims; the impact of contemporaneous events; the degree of control the Nazis had on a country or local popu-lation; the cultural attitudes of particular native populations historically toward different victim groups, and the availability, effectiveness, and risk of potential hiding places.

Students should be reminded that individuals and groups do not always fit neatly into the same categories of behavior. The very same people did not always act consistently as "bystanders," "col-laborators," "perpetrators," or "rescuers." Individuals and groups often behaved differently depending upon changing events and circum-stances. The same person who in 1933 might have stood by and remained uninvolved while wit-nessing social discrimination of Jews, might later have joined up with the SA and become a collab-orator or have been moved to dissent vocally or act in defense of Jewish friends and neighbors.

Encourage your students not to categorize groups of people only on the basis of their experi-ences during the Holocaust: contextualization is critical so that victims are not perceived only as victims. Although Jews were the central victims of the Nazi regime, they had a vibrant culture and long history in Europe prior to the Nazi era. By exposing students to some of the cultural contri-butions and achievements of two thousand years of European Jewish life, you help students to bal-ance their perception of Jews as victims and to better appreciate the traumatic disruption in Jewish history caused by the Holocaust.

Similarly, students may know very little about Gypsies, except for the negative images and derogatory descriptions promulgated by the Nazis. Students would benefit from a broader viewpoint, learning something about Gypsy his-tory and culture, and understanding the diverse ways of life among different Gypsy groups.

10. Translate statistics into people.

In any study of the Holocaust, the sheer number of victims challenges easy comprehension. Teachers need to show that individual people are behind the statistics, comprised of families of grandparents, parents, and children. First-person accounts and

memoir literature provide students with a way of making meaning out of collective numbers. Although students should be careful about over-generalizing from first-person accounts such as those from survivors, journalists, relief workers, bystanders, and liberators, personal accounts can supplement a study of genocide by moving it "from a welter of statistics, remote places and events, to one that is immersed in the 'personal' and 'particular.'" [Totten, 1987, p. 63]

11. Be sensitive to appropriate written and audio-visual content.

One of the primary concerns of educators is how to introduce students to the horrors of the Holocaust. Graphic material should be used in a judicious manner and only to the extent neces-sary to achieve the objective of the lesson. Teachers should remind themselves that each stu-dent and each class is different, and that what seems appropriate for one may not be for all.

Students are essentially a "captive audience." When we assault them with images of horror for which they are unprepared, we violate a basic trust: the obligation of a teacher to provide a "safe" learning environment. The assumption that all students will seek to understand human behav-ior after being exposed to horrible images is falla-cious. Some students may be so appalled by images of brutality and mass murder that they are discouraged from studying the subject further; oth-ers may become fascinated in a more voyeuristic fashion, subordinating further critical analysis of the history to the superficial titillation of looking at images of starvation, disfigurement, and death. Many events and deeds that occurred within the context of the Holocaust do not rely for their depiction directly on the graphic horror of mass killings or other barbarisms. It is recommended that images and texts that do not exploit either the vic-tims' memories or the students' emotional vulnera-bility form the centerpiece of Holocaust curricula.

12. Strive for balance in establishing whose perspec-tive informs your study of the Holocaust.

Often, too great an emphasis is placed on the vic-tims of Nazi aggression, rather than on the vic-timizers who forced people to make impossible choices or simply left them with no choice to make. Most students express empathy for victims of mass murder. But, it is not uncommon for stu-dents to assume that the victims may have done something to justify the actions against them, and thus to place inappropriate blame on the vic-tims themselves.

There is also a tendency among students to glorify power, even when it is used to kill inno-cent people. Many teachers indicate that their students are intrigued and in some cases, intellec-tually seduced, by the symbols of power which pervaded Nazi propaganda (e.g., the swastika, Nazi flags and regalia, Nazi slogans, rituals, and music). Rather than highlight the trappings of Nazi power, teachers should ask students to eval-uate how such elements are used by govern-ments (including our own) to build, protect, and mobilize a society. Students should be encour-aged to contemplate as well how such elements can be abused and manipulated by governments to implement and legitimize acts of terror and even genocide.

In any review of the propaganda used to pro-mote Nazi ideology, Nazi stereotypes of targeted victim groups, and the Hitler regime's justifications for persecution and murder, teachers need to remind students that just because such policies and beliefs are under discussion in class does not mean they are acceptable. It would be a terrible irony if students arrived at such a conclusion.

Furthermore, any study of the Holocaust should address both the victims and the perpetra-tors of violence, and attempt to portray each as human beings, capable of moral judgment and independent decision-making but challenged by circumstances which made both self-defense and independent thought not merely difficult but perilous and potentially lethal.

13. Select appropriate learning activities.

Just because students favor a certain learning activity does not necessarily mean that it should be used. For example, such activities as word scrambles, crossword puzzles, and other gimmicky exercises tend not to encourage critical analysis, but lead instead to low level types of thinking and, in the case of Holocaust curricula, trivialize the importance of studying this history. When the effects of a particular activity run counter to the rationale for studying the history, then that activity should not be used.

Similarly, activities that encourage students to construct models of killing camps should also be reconsidered since any assignment along this line will almost inevitably end up being simplistic, time-consuming, and tangential to the educational objectives for studying the history of the Holocaust.

Thought-provoking learning activities are preferred, but even here, there are pitfalls to avoid. In studying complex human behavior, many teachers rely upon simulation exercises meant to help students "experience" unfamiliar situations. Even when teachers take great care to prepare a class for such an activity, simulating experiences from the Holocaust remains pedagogically unsound. The activity may engage students, but they often forget the purpose of the lesson, and even worse, they are left with the impression at the conclusion of the activity that they now know what it was like during the Holocaust.

Holocaust survivors and eyewitnesses are among the first to indicate the grave difficulty of finding words to describe their experiences. Even more revealing, they argue the virtual impossibility of trying to simulate accurately what it was like

to live on a daily basis with fear, hunger, disease, unfathomable loss, and the unrelenting threat of abject brutality and death.

The problem with trying to simulate situations from the Holocaust is that complex events and actions are over-simplified, and students are left with a skewed view of history. Since there are numerous primary source accounts, both written and visual, as well as survivors and eyewitnesses who can describe actual choices faced and made by individuals, groups, and nations during this period, teachers should draw upon these resources and refrain from simulation games that lead to a trivialization of the subject matter.

If they are not attempting to re-create situations from the Holocaust, simulation activities can be used effectively, especially when they have been designed to explore varying aspects of human behavior such as fear, scapegoating, conflict resolution, and difficult decision-making. Asking students in the course of a discussion, or as part of a writing assignment, to consider various perspectives on a particular event or historical experience is fundamentally different from involving a class in a simulation game.

14. Reinforce the objectives of your lesson plan.

As in all teaching situations, the opening and closing lessons are critically important. A strong opening should serve to dispel misinformation students may have prior to studying the Holocaust. It should set a reflective tone, move students from passive to active learners, indicate to students that their ideas and opinions matter, and establish that this history has multiple ramifications for themselves as individuals and as members of society as a whole.

A strong closing should emphasize synthesis by encouraging students to connect this history to other world events as well as the world they live in today. Students should be encouraged to reflect on what they have learned and to consider what this study means to them personally and as citizens of a democracy. Most importantly, your closing lesson should encourage further examination of Holocaust history, literature, and art.

Incorporating a Study of the Holocaust into Existing Courses

The Holocaust can be effectively integrated into various existing courses within the school curriculum. This section presents sample rationale statements and methodological approaches for incorporating a study of the Holocaust in seven different courses. Each course synopsis constitutes a mere fraction of the various rationales and approaches currently used by educators. Often, the rationales and methods listed under one course can be applied as well to other courses.

United States History

Although the history of the United States is introduced at various grade levels throughout most school curricula, all states require students to take a course in United States history at the high school level. Including a study of the Holocaust into U.S. History courses can encourage students to:

- examine the dilemmas that arise when foreign policy goals are narrowly defined, as solely in terms of the national interest, thus denying the validity of universal moral and human priorities;
- understand what happens when parliamentary democratic institutions fail;
- examine the responses of governmental and non-governmental organizations in the United States to the plight of Holocaust victims (e.g., the Evian Conference, the debate over the Wagner-Rogers bill to assist refugee children, the ill-fated voyage of the S.S. St. Louis, the Emergency Rescue Committee, the rallies and efforts of Rabbi Stephen S. Wise, and the decision by the U.S. not to bomb the railroad lines leading into Auschwitz);

- explore the role of American and Allied soldiers in liberating victims from Nazi concentration camps and killing centers, using, for example, first-person accounts of liberators to ascertain their initial responses to, and subsequent reflections about, what they witnessed; and
- examine the key role played by the U.S. in bringing Nazi perpetrators to trial at Nuremberg and in other war crimes trials.

Since most history and social studies teachers in the United States rely upon standard textbooks, they can incorporate the Holocaust into regular units of study such as the Great Depression, World War II, and the Cold War. Questions which introduce Holocaust studies into these subject areas include:

The Great Depression:

How did the U.S. respond to the Depression? How were U.S. electoral politics influenced by the Depression? What were the immediate consequences of the Depression on the European economic and political system established by the Versailles Treaty of 1919? What was the impact of the Depression upon the electoral strength of the Nazi party in Germany? Was the Depression a contributing factor to the Nazis' rise to power?

World War II:

What was the relationship between the U.S. and Nazi Germany from 1933 to 1939? How did the actions of Nazi Germany influence U.S. foreign policy? What was the response of the U.S. Government and non-governmental organizations to the unfolding events of the Holocaust? What was the role of the U.S. in the war crimes trials?

The Cold War:

How did the rivalries between the World War II allies influence American attitudes toward former Nazis?

What was the position of America's European allies toward members of the former Nazi regime?

World History

Although various aspects of world history are incorporated throughout school curricula, most students are not required to take World History courses. It is in the context of World History courses, however, that the Holocaust is generally taught. Inclusion of the Holocaust in a World History course helps students to:

- examine events, deeds, and ideas in European history that contributed to the Holocaust, such as the history of antisemitism in Europe, 19th century race science, the rise of German nationalism, the defeat of Germany in World War I, and the failure of the Weimar Republic to govern successfully;

- reflect upon the idea that civilization has been progressing [one possible exercise might be to have students develop a definition of "civilization" in class, and then have them compare and contrast Nazi claims for the "1000 Year Reich" with the actual policies they employed to realize that vision; the dissonance raised in such a lesson helps students to see that government policies can encompass evil, particularly when terror and brute force crush dissent];

- explore how the various policies of the Nazi regime were interrelated (e.g., the connections between establishing a totalitarian government, carrying out racial policies, and waging war); and

- reflect upon the moral and ethical implications of the Nazi era as a watershed in world history (e.g., the systematic planning and implementation of a government policy to kill millions of people; the use of technological advances to carry out mass slaughter; the role of Nazi collaborators, and the role of bystanders around the world who chose not to intervene in the persecution and murder of Jews and other victims).

Once again, since most teachers of European history rely upon standard textbooks and a chronological approach, teachers may wish to incorporate the Holocaust into the following, standardized units of study in European History: the Aftermath of World War I; the Rise of Dictators; the World at War, 1939–45, and the Consequences of War. Questions which introduce Holocaust studies into these subject areas include:

The Aftermath of World War I:

What role did the Versailles Treaty play in the restructuring of European and world politics? How did the reconfiguration of Europe following World War I influence German national politics in the period 1919–33?

The Rise of the Dictators:

What factors led to the rise of totalitarian regimes in Europe in the period between the two world wars? How was antisemitism used by the Nazis and other regimes (Hungary, Romania, U.S.S.R.) to justify totalitarian measures?

The World at War, 1939–45:

Why has the Holocaust often been called a "war within the war?" How did the Holocaust affect Nazi military decisions? Why might it be "easier" to commit genocidal acts during wartime than during a period of relative peace?

The Consequences of War:

What was the connection between World War II and the formation of the State of Israel? Was a new strain of international morality introduced with the convening of the Nuremberg Tribunals? How did the Cold War impact the fate of former Nazis?

World Cultures

A course on World Cultures incorporates knowledge from both the humanities and the social sciences into a study of cultural patterns and social institutions of various societies. A study of the Holocaust in a World Cultures course helps students:

- examine conflicts arising between majority and minority groups in a specific cultural sphere (Europe between 1933–45);
- further their understanding of how a government can use concepts such as culture, ethnicity, race, diversity, and nationality as weapons to persecute, murder, and annihilate people;
- analyze the extent to which cultures are able to survive and maintain their traditions and institutions, when faced with threats to their very existence (e.g., retaining religious practices, recording eyewitness accounts, and hiding cultural symbols and artifacts); and
- apply understandings gleaned from an examination of the Holocaust to genocides which have occurred in other cultural spheres.

Government

Government courses at the high school level usually focus on understanding the U.S. political system, comparative studies of various governments, and the international relationship of nations. The Holocaust can be incorporated into a study of government in order to demonstrate how the development of public policy can become directed to genocidal ends when dissent and debate are silenced. Inclusion of Holocaust studies in Government courses helps students:

- compare governmental systems (e.g., by investigating how the Weimar Constitution in Germany prior to the Nazi seizure of power was similar to, or different from, the Constitution of the United States; by comparing the Nazi system of governance with that of the United States);

- study the process of how a state can degenerate from a (parliamentary) democracy into a totalitarian state (e.g., by examining the processes by which the Nazis gained absolute control of the German government and how the Nazi government then controlled virtually all segments of German society);
- examine how the development of public policy can lead to genocidal ends, especially when people remain silent in face of discriminatory practices (e.g., the development of Nazi racial and genocide policies towards Jews and other victim groups beginning with the philosophical platform elaborated in Hitler's Mein Kampf, continuing through the state-imposed Nuremberg Laws, and culminating with governmental policies of murder and extermination after 1941);
- examine the role of Nazi bureaucracy in implementing policies of murder and annihilation (e.g., the development and maintenance of a system to identify, isolate, deport, enslave, and kill targeted people, and then redistribute their remaining belongings);
- examine the role of various individuals in the rise and fall of a totalitarian government (e.g., those who supported Nazi Germany, those who were passive, and those who resisted both internally, such as partisans and others who carried out revolts, and externally, such as the Allies; and
- recognize that among the legacies of the Holocaust have been the creation of the United Nations in 1945, and its ongoing efforts to develop and adopt numerous, significant human rights bills (e.g., the U.N. Declaration of Human Rights and the U.N. Convention on Genocide).

Contemporary World Problems

Many schools include a Contemporary World Problems course at the senior high level which allows students to conduct an in-depth study of a topic such as genocide. The focus is usually on what constitutes genocide, and areas of investigation include various preconditions, patterns, consequences, and methods of intervention and prevention of genocide. A study of the Holocaust in Contemporary World Problems curricula can help students to:

- comprehend the similarities and differences between governmental policies during the Holocaust and contemporary policies that create the potential for ethnocide or genocide (e.g., comparing and contrasting the philosophy and/or policies of the Nazi regime with that of the Khmer Rouge in Cambodia);

- compare and contrast the world response of governments and non-governmental organizations to the Holocaust with the responses of governments and non-governmental organizations to mass killings today (e.g., comparing the decisions made at the Evian Conference in 1938, to the U.S. response to the Cambodian genocide between 1974–1979, or the response of non-governmental organizations like the International Red Cross to the Nazi genocide of Jews during the Holocaust with that of Amnesty International to political killings in Argentina, Guatemala, Indonesia, and Cambodia in contemporary times); and

- analyze the relationship of the Holocaust and its legacy to the formation of the State of Israel.

Literature

Literature is read in English classes across grade levels and is also used to enhance and strengthen social studies and science courses. The literature curriculum is generally organized thematically or around categories such as American Literature, British Literature, European Literature, and World Literature. Literature, is capable of providing thought-provoking perspectives on a myriad of subjects and concerns which can engage students in ways that standard textbooks and essays do not.

Holocaust literature encompasses a variety of literary genres including novels, short stories, drama, poetry, diaries, and memoirs. This broad spectrum gives teachers a wide range of curriculum choices.

Because Holocaust literature derives from a true-to-life epic in human history, its stories reveal basic truths about human nature, and provide adolescent readers with credible models of heroism and dignity. At the same time, it compels them to confront the reality of the human capacity for evil.

Because so many of the stories intersect with issues in students' own lives, Holocaust literature can inspire a commitment to reject indifference to human suffering, and can instruct them about relevant social issues such as the effects of intolerance and elitism. Studying literary responses to the Holocaust helps students:

- develop a deeper respect for human decency by asking them to confront the moral depravity and the extent of Nazi evil (e.g., the abject cruelty of the Nazi treatment of victims even prior to the round-ups and deportations; the event of Kristallnacht; the deportations in boxcars; the mass killings; and the so-called medical experiments of Nazi doctors);

- recognize the deeds of heroism demonstrated by teenagers and adults in ghettos and concentration camps (e.g., the couriers who smuggled messages, goods, and weapons in and out of the Warsaw Ghetto; the partisans who used arms to resist the Nazis; the uprisings and revolts in various ghettos including Warsaw and in killing centers such as Treblinka);

- explore the spiritual resistance evidenced in literary responses which portray the irrepressible dignity of people who transcended the evil of their murderers, as found, for example, in the clandestine writing of diaries, poetry, and plays;

- recognize the different roles which were assumed or thrust upon people during the Holocaust, such as victim, oppressor, bystander, and rescuer;

- examine the moral choices, or absence of choices, which were confronted by both young and old, victim and perpetrator; and

- analyze the corruption of language cultivated by the Nazis, particularly in the use of euphemisms to

mask their evil intent (e.g., their use of the terms "emigration" for expulsion, "evacuation" for deportation, "deportation" for transportation to concentration camps and killing centers, "police actions" for round-ups that typically led to mass murder, and "Final Solution" for the planned annihilation of every Jew in Europe).

Art and Art History

One of the goals for studying art history is to enable students to understand the role of art in society. The Holocaust can be incorporated into a study of art and art history to illuminate how the Nazis used art for propagandistic purposes, and how victims used artistic expression to communicate their protest, despair, and/or hope. A study of art during the Holocaust helps students:

- analyze the motivations for, and implications of, the Nazi's censorship activities in the fine and literary arts, theater, and music (e.g., the banning of books and certain styles of painting; the May 1933 book burnings);
- examine the values and beliefs of the Nazis and how the regime perceived the world, by, for example, examining Nazi symbols of power, Nazi propaganda posters, paintings, and drawings deemed "acceptable" rather than "degenerate";
- study how people living under Nazi control used art as a form of resistance (e.g., examining the

extent to which the victims created art; the dangers they faced in doing so; the various forms of art that were created and the settings in which they were created, and the diversity of themes and content in this artistic expression);

- examine art created by Holocaust victims and survivors and explore its capacity to document diverse experiences including life prior to the Holocaust, life inside the ghettos, the deportations, and the myriad of experiences in the concentration camp system; and
- examine interpretations of the Holocaust as expressed in contemporary art, art exhibitions, and memorials.

Conclusion

A study of the Holocaust can be effectively integrated into any number of subject areas. Sample curricula and lesson plans, currently in use around the country, have been collected by the United States Holocaust Memorial Museum and are available for reference purposes. For further information on the range of materials available, and how to acquire copies of these materials for your own use in developing or enhancing study units on the Holocaust, please contact the Education Department, United States Holocaust Memorial Museum, 100 Raoul Wallenberg Place, SW, Washington, DC 20024; telephone: (202) 488-0400.

References

Oliner, Pearl M. and Samuel P. Oliner. "Righteous People in the Holocaust." Genocide: A Critical Bibliographic Review. Edited by Israel Charny. London and New York: Mansell Publishing and Facts on File, respectively, 1991.

Totten, Samuel. "The Personal Face of Genocide: Words of Witnesses in the Classroom." Special Issue of the Social Science Record ("Genocide: Issues, Approaches, Resources") 24, 2 (1987): 63–67.

Acknowledgments

Primary authors:

William S. Parsons, Director of Education & Visitor Services, U.S. Holocaust Memorial Museum (U.S.H.M.M.); and Samuel Totten, Assistant Professor of Curriculum and Instruction, University of Arkansas, Fayetteville

We would also like to acknowledge editorial suggestions made by:

Helen Fagin, Chair, U.S. Holocaust Memorial Council Education Committee;

Sara J. Bloomfield, Associate Museum Director for Public Programs;

Alice M. Greenwald, Consultant (U.S.H.M.M.);

Stephen Feinberg, Social Studies Department Chairman, Wayland Middle School, Wayland, MA;

William R. Fernekes, Social Studies Supervisor, Hunterdon Central Regional High School, Flemington, NJ;

Grace M. Caporino, Advanced Placement English Teacher, Carmel High School, Carmel, NY; and

Kristy L. Brosius, Resource Center Coordinator (U.S.H.M.M.).